NICARAGUAN SKETCHES

JULIO CORTÁZAR

WORKS IN ENGLISH TRANSLATION

The Winners (1965)

Hopscotch (1966)

The End of the Game and Other Stories (1967)

Cronopios and Famas (1969)

62: A Model Kit (1972)

All Fires the Fire and Other Stories (1973)

A Manual for Manuel (1978)

A Change of Light and Other Stories (1980)

We Love Glenda So Much and Other Tales (1983)

A Certain Lucas (1984)

Around the Day in Eighty Worlds (1986)

Nicaraguan Sketches (1989)

Julio Cortázar

Nicaraguan
Sketches

TRANSLATED BY
KATHLEEN WEAVER

W. W. NORTON & COMPANY

NEW YORK   LONDON

The text of this book is composed in 12/15 Bodoni Book,
with display type set in Latin Elongated.
Composition and manufacturing by the Haddon Craftsmen, Inc.
Book design by Margaret Wagner.

First Edition

Library of Congress Cataloging-in-Publication Data
Cortázar, Julio.
[Nicaragua tan violentamente dulce. English]
Nicaraguan sketches / by Julio Cortázar;
translated by Kathleen Weaver.
p. cm.
Fifteen essays written between 1976 and 1983.
Translation of: Nicaragua tan violentamente dulce.
1. Nicaragua—History–1979–I. Title.
F1528.C6713 1989
972.8505'3—dc20   89-32268

ISBN 0-393-02764-3

W. W. Norton & Company, Inc.
500 Fifth Avenue, New York, N. Y. 10110
W. W. Norton & Company Ltd.
37 Great Russell Street, London WC1B 3NU

1 2 3 4 5 6 7 8 9 0

For the FSLN

Contents

Translator's Acknowledgments

I *WOULD* like to acknowledge, with gratitude, the assistance of Bob Baldock, whose extensive editing and rewriting, especially of the initial chapter, and his encouragement throughout, have greatly benefited this translation. The assistance of Judy Wilkinson, which amounted to a thorough collaboration on the final revision of the text, is also deeply appreciated. I am thankful to Bernardo García-Pandavenes, who generously helped interpret many passages in Cortázar's Spanish, and finally, I would like to thank Bill Rusin, of W. W. Norton, for his support for this project and his work to bring it to completion.

The text is based on the Nicaraguan edition of *Nicaragua tan violentamente dulce,* with the omission of Cortázar's introductory poem.

Translator's Introduction

IN 1968 Sandinista leader Doris Tijerino was in Managua, desperately in need of a place to hide for a few days, to escape the agents of Somoza's security force. She was given the name of a woman who lived in one of the poorest barrios in the city, near the lake. This woman took her in without asking questions. Tijerino describes the poverty she encountered:

> She was poor, extremely poor. She didn't have a steady job and lived by peddling. She'd sell vegetables one day, fruit the next, used clothes and old shoes another. And she had a lot of children, seven or eight. The oldest was about twelve.
>
> They had a very small house with only one room. There was no drinking water. As these houses are situated near the lake, they sink a shallow well and the water filtering in from the lake is what they drink. That water is very dirty because all the polluted water from the city drains into Lake Managua. As a result the water has a layer of greenish scum on top.
>
> The mother and her companion, who wasn't the father of most of her children, would go out to work very early. The children would stay alone and were the responsibility of the oldest girl,

who was twelve. A smaller girl of nine had to do the cooking because the twelve year old had to go out too—from house to house to find someone who might need her services as a laundress. She'd do a little washing and with what she earned she bought a few beans, the only thing they ate all day. . . .

There was no kitchen but they made a *tenamaste*—three big stones, with firewood in the middle and on top the casserole to cook in. Every time one of the little ones was hungry, she was served a few spoonfuls of what was in the pot, it was put in the child's hand or on a leaf. Of course the children had diarrhea all the time. The house smelled of excrement. It was horrible.

There was a boy of two who hadn't been bathed in who knows how long . . . probably not since he was born. His whole body was covered with pimples, and it seemed as if he wasn't going to be able to hear. . . .

They didn't have a toilet either, much less a bathroom. They had to attend to the calls of nature at the side of the house or squat behind a bush. The little nine year old girl in charge of the cooking had something the matter with one eye, like a tumor. The eye was closed and useless. . . .

They were very intelligent children.[1]

Although Julio Cortázar does not portray such conditions in detail in his writings on Nicaragua, he constantly alludes to the persistence of this poverty, a misery and oppression he came increasingly to protest—as an outspoken supporter of the liberation movements of Latin America.

Cortázar arrived at this position gradually, by a paradoxical circumnavigation: he approached Latin America by moving away from it, to Europe. As Eduardo Galeano writes in his trilogy, *Memories of Fire,* Cortázar went forward by going back. "He went from the end toward the beginning; from discouragement to enthusiasm, from indifference to passion, from solitude to solidarity."[2]

Cortázar was born in 1914 in Brussels, where his father was an Argentine diplomat; in 1918 his parents returned with their son to Argentina, where Cortázar grew up near Buenos Aires, one of the most Europeanized cities in Latin America.

In 1951 Cortázar made the decision to leave Argentina to make a life for himself in France. He settled in Paris, where he lived for over thirty years, working as a translator for the United Nations.

Though repeatedly criticized for his voluntary expatriation—for living comfortably in Europe while speaking out on behalf of the poor of Latin America—Cortázar refused to apologize for living in Paris, a city he felt ideally suited to his tastes and temperament. He continually defended what he perceived as the gain in perspective, the wider vision afforded by his distance from Latin America. Furthermore, he insisted, his concern for Latin America was an ethical concern, as much European as Latin American; it had nothing to do with the address on his passport.

Cortázar was a writer of genuine erudition, with a tremendous breadth of interests and sympathies. He had, for example, an intricate knowledge of jazz, which he loved. His writings, sometimes thought difficult, even arcane, and full of linguistic playfulness, won Cortázar devoted readers from the very beginning of his career.

The publication of Cortázar's *Rayuela* (Hopscotch), in 1963, brought him international attention. This experimental "antinovel", which could be entered like a labyrinth, and read in a variety of sequences, had a particularly strong impact in Latin America, where it is generally acknowledged to

be a key work in the twentieth-century literature of that continent. While of an older generation than either Gabriel García
Márquez or Carlos Fuentes, Cortázar is invariably grouped
with them as a creator of the "boom" in Latin American
fiction.

García Márquez, who admired Cortázar's early work,
remembers seeing him for the first time, in Paris, in late
October 1956. He had heard that Cortázar frequented the Old
Navy cafe on the Boulevard Saint-Germain. For several
weeks García Márquez waited, hoping Cortázar would appear,
and finally he did:

> Like an apparition. He was the tallest man you could possibly
> imagine, wearing a voluminous black raincoat which was more
> like the dark cloak of a widow. His face was the face of a per-
> verse child: wide-set eyes like those of a heifer, so oblique and
> filmy they might have seemed diabolical had they not been sub-
> mitted to the dominion of the heart.[3]

García Márquez never dared to approach him that day, as
Cortázar sat at a corner table, writing in a school notebook for
over an hour without stopping, not even pausing, drinking
nothing but half a glass of mineral water. Finally, when it was
getting dark, Cortázar put his pen into his bag and walked
out, notebook under his arm, "the tallest and thinnest student
in the world."

Cuban author José Lezama Lima suggested that Cortázar
had received the gift of eternal youth in exchange for never
being able to stop growing taller. (Cortázar was around six
feet six inches tall.) His exceptionally youthful appearance
was often mentioned. Tc those who knew him it seemed he

grew steadily younger, as though physically mirroring his own youthful spirit.

In 1959 Fidel Castro's 26th of July Movement overthrew dictator Fulgencio Batista in Cuba. Artists and writers from all over the world, but particularly Latin Americans, were invited to visit the island and see for themselves what the Cuban Revolution was trying to do. Cortázar first traveled to Cuba in 1961, a particularly intense moment in Cuban history. In three extraordinary days in April the young revolution had defeated the mercenary invasion at the Bay of Pigs, and Fidel had delivered his emotional Declaration of Havana, announcing the definitively socialist character of the revolution—"a revolution of the humble, by the humble, and for the humble." The literacy campaign was underway. For Cortázar this was a profound experience, a decisive one, a turning point in his voyage of discovery, in his journey from the New World to the Old, now back to the New. That huge gulf between the Europe of cosmopolitan Paris and the narrow world of Cortázar's Argentine boyhood had been bridged by the international socialism of Cuba. His socialist conviction, before vague and intellectual, now deepened into a principle of action.

Cortázar was fully aware of the irony of having to go to Europe "to discover a little of the real roots of what is Latin American."[4] For Cortázar, returning to Latin America did not mean the recovery of a nationality or of a folklore; rather it meant the reconciliation of the Old World and the New, of the European and the Latin American within himself.

"A writer left Argentina who thought that reality should end in a book," Cortázar noted. "In Paris a writer was born who thought books should end in reality."[5]

Following a second trip to Cuba several years later, Cortázar made a conscious decision to speak out as a writer, to identify himself more consistently and actively with the cause of socialism and with the liberation movements of Latin America. At the same time he vowed to pursue his own literary course with full imaginative freedom.

In a beautiful long letter written in 1967 to his friend Roberto Fernández Retamar, editor of the Cuban literary journal *Casa de las Americas,* Cortázar writes of his political evolution: "I no longer believe, as I once could, so comfortably, that literature of mere imaginative creation is sufficient to make me feel that I have fulfilled myself as a writer."[6]

Living in Europe, he acknowledged to Retamar, it would not be easy to maintain a committed stance:

> The slow, absorbing, infinite and egotistic traffic with beauty and culture—life on a continent where a few hours put me in front of a fresco by Giotto or a Velazquez at the Prado . . . or in those London galleries where the paintings of Turner seem to reinvent light, the daily temptation to return as in other days to a total, feverish absorption in intellectual and aesthetic problems, to lofty games of thought and imagination, to creativity with no other finality than the pleasure of the intellect or the senses—all this sets off in me an interminable battle with the feeling that none of it is justified if at the same time it is not open to the vital problems.[7]

Immediately following the electoral victory of the Popular Unity government in Chile, in 1970, Cortázar flew to Santiago and was received by President Salvador Allende. He visited the shanty town being rebuilt as Población Pablo Neruda, while its streets were being sketched out in dirt and given the names of Neruda poems. Three years later, after the bloody coup which killed Allende and brought Pinochet to power, Cortázar met in Paris with García Márquez and Chilean writers Volodia Teitelboim and Ariel Dorfman to discuss what they might do, concretely and immediately, on behalf of Chile. García Márquez vowed to cease writing novels until Pinochet was overthrown; he would instead devote himself to journalism. Cortázar made no vow to abandon fiction but began at once to denounce the Pinochet regime. The Videla coup, which brought the military to power in Argentina, led to equally urgent demands upon his time. In response to events in Latin America, Cortázar's political involvement grew.

Cortázar wrote in 1979 to Haydée Santamaría of Casa de las Americas in Havana to say that he and his second wife Ugné Karvelis had amicably separated and that he would be bringing Carol Dunlop, a young writer and his future wife, with him to Cuba on his coming trip.

Following a clandestine trip to Nicaragua to visit Ernesto Cardenal's religious community of Solentiname, Cortázar became a vocal supporter of the Sandinista's fight against Somoza. Three years later, in what Cortázar calls a "prodigious acceleration of history," Somoza was in Miami and the Sandinista revolution had triumphed (July 19, 1979). Cortázar immediately made plans to go to Nicaragua.

When Comandante Tomás Borge heard of these plans he immediately declared that Julio and Carol Dunlop would stay with him. The only surviving founder of the FSLN, and a legendary hero in Nicaragua, Borge, probably more than anyone else, has been responsible for encouraging the alliance of Christians and Marxists in the Sandinista revolution. Imprisoned under Somoza, brutally tortured, and held for long periods in solitary confinement, Borge was personally grateful to Cortázar for having written books that meant a great deal to him while in prison. Whenever the couple was in Nicaragua, they stayed at Borge's home. There was talk of making Nicaragua their future base, but the precarious health of Carol, and also of Julio, precluded this eventuality.

One night, Borge recalls, "Carol took me aside to speak in private. She had been experiencing sharp pains in her bones. With hands full of mystery and gentle eyes, she confided to me the secret that she had only a few more months to live."[8]

The couple returned abruptly to Paris, where Carol Dunlop died in November of 1982. Cortázar was devastated with grief, from which it is said he never fully recovered. Borge describes his concern for his friend:

> I feared his return to our house. I knew he would be back, but without Carol, and I feared that our house, the familiar atmosphere, the landscape of the country, would be painful, would intensify his grief. But he reappeared, and I saw the same Cortázar as before. It seemed to us that his love was what consoled him . . . Grief is sometimes accompanied by remorse, but for Cortázar, who loved his compañera so completely, and who knew how to express that love, this was not a problem. His devotion to Carol reflected his ability to give of himself to others.[9]

Cortázar returned to Nicaragua in 1983 and resumed his activities with a vengeance. Disregarding his own safety he traveled to the war zone with the Vigil for Peace. From there he went directly to Managua to receive Nicaragua's highest honor, the Rubén Darío Award.

In the fall of 1983, in an interview for a Spanish television program, he spoke of his desire to begin a novel and of his hope that the next year might be "a sabbatical year."[10] But other things continued to be more pressing. With the end of the military dictatorship in Argentina and the inauguration of the civilian government of Raúl Alfonsín, it became possible for Cortázar to fly to Bueno Aires after a political exile of ten years. While in Argentina, after a brief stay, his deteriorating health forced him to return to Paris and his apartment on the rue Martel. He continued working, collecting his articles on Argentina and finishing the editing of his poems. Compiling these poems of a lifetime, Cortázar noted that he was able to date the undated ones not by themes, which remained more or less the same, but by vocabulary and degree of abstraction. The earlier the poem, the more abstract. "It is not that I am seeking out the concrete," he wrote, "but the concrete, I think, is seeking out me, and—it seems to have found me."[11]

Shortly before his death from leukemia in February, 1984, his collection of articles on Nicaragua, *Nicaragua tan violentamente dulce,* was published in Managua. All author's proceeds from this work were to be donated to the Sandinistas.

NOTES

1. Doris Tijerino, *Inside the Nicaraguan Revolution,* as told to Margaret Randall, trans. Elinor Randall (Vancouver: New Star Books, 1978).
2. Eduardo Galeano, *Memories of Fire,* vol. 3, *Century of the Wind,* trans. Cedric Belfrage (New York: Pantheon, 1988), p. 276 (translation slightly revised).
3. Gabriel García Márquez, "El argentino que se hizo querer de todos," *Casa de las Americas,* nos. 145–46 (July–August 1984): 23.
4. Julio Cortázar, "Letter to Roberto Fernández Retamar, May 10, 1967," trans.

Jo Anne Engelbert, in *Lives on the Line: The Testimony of Contemporary Latin American Authors,* ed. Doris Meyer (Berkeley: University of California Press, 1988), p. 77.

5. Ibid., p. 78.
6. Ibid., p. 81.
7. Ibid., p. 82.
8. Tomás Borge, "Julio Cortázar, compañero de prisión y libertad," in Sergio Ramírez et al., *Queremos tanto a Julio,* ed. Hugo Niño (Managua: Ediciones Nueva Nicaragua, 1984), p. 37.
9. Ibid., p. 38.
10. Julio Cortázar, Ernesto Cardenal, and Ricardo Utrilla, interviewed by Mercedes Milá, on "Buenas Noches," Spanish Television, November 24, 1983, in Julio Cortázar, *Nicaragua tan violentamente dulce* (Barcelona: Muchnik Ediciones, 1984), p. 133.
11. Victor Rodríguez Núñez, quoting Julio Cortázar's notes to *Salvo el crepúsculo,* in "Salvo el crepúsculo: Salvo la poesía," *Casa de las Americas,* nos. 145–46 (July–August 1984): 248.

NICARAGUAN SKETCHES

Apocalypse in Solentiname

T*HE* Costa Ricans—the Ticos—are rather quiet, but full of
surprises. I land in San José and there awaiting me are Carmen Naranjo,* Samuel Rovinski,* and Sergio Ramírez* (who
is not a Tico but a Nicaraguan, but what does it matter since
it's all the same? What does it matter if I'm an Argentine?
Though to be truly informal I should call myself a Tino, and
the others Nicas and Ticos). Anyway, the heat was staggering,
and to make matters even worse things started off immediately with the usual press conference and the usual questions:
"Why don't you live in your own country?" "Why was the
film *Blow Up* so different from your story?" "Is it your opinion that the writer should be politically engaged?" I might as
well face it—my last interview will be at the gates of hell. I'm
absolutely certain that the questions will be the same. And if
by any chance I end up *chez* Saint Peter, it won't be any
different. "Mr. Cortázar," they'll say, "don't you think that
down on earth your writing was a bit too difficult for the
ordinary reader?"

At last the Hotel Europa and that shower which finishes off
all my trips with a long monologue of soap and silence. By

*Asterisks refer the reader to the Notes section.

seven that evening I was ready to take a walk through San
José, to see if it really was as simple and neatly ordered as I'd
been told. As I was leaving the hotel a hand tugged at my
jacket and I turned to find Ernesto Cardenal.* What an em-
brace, poet! How good to see you here after our meeting in
Rome, and after so many meetings—on paper—over the
years. I'm always surprised, always touched, that someone
like Ernesto should seek me out, should come to meet me.
You may say this smacks of false modesty, but say what you
will, my friend: the jackal howls, but the bus goes right on by.
I'll always be an admirer, somebody who loves certain people
so much, however distant they may be, until one day it turns
out they love him, too. Things like this overwhelm me, so let's
move on to what comes next.

Which is this: Ernesto had been informed by one of his
little birds that the Ticos were planning a trip for me to Solentiname* (his home island in Nicaragua), and he couldn't resist
the idea of flying in to collect me himself.

Two days later, Sergio, Oscar, Ernesto and I crowded into
the all-too-crowdable cabin of a Piper Aztec plane (why it's
called that I'll never know). It flew amid metallic hiccoughs
and ominous internal rattlings, which the blond pilot tried to
drown out by turning on some loud calypso; he remained
completely indifferent to my concern that the Aztec might be
taking us straight to some pyramid of sacrifice.

We landed in Los Chiles, near the Nicaraguan border.
From there an equally bumpy jeep took us on to the farm of
José Coronel Urtecho* (a poet more people would do well to
read). We rested in his house, talking about other poet
friends—Roque Dalton,* Gertrude Stein, and Carlos Mar-

tínez Rivas*—until Luis Coronel came to take us in his jeep, then in his lurching speedboat, into Nicaragua.

But first there were snapshots with one of those cameras that eject a rectangle of pale blue paper which little by little in a Polaroid marvel gradually fills with an image, first ectoplasmic and disturbing, then gradually a nose, curly hair, and finally you have Ernesto smiling from under his Nazarene headband, and Doña Maria and Don José on the veranda, partly out of the frame. To everybody else, this seemed perfectly natural, for they were used to that camera. But for me, as I told them all, to see faces and smiles emerging from that pale blue blankness was simply astonishing. I remember asking Oscar what would happen if a typical family snapshot, suddenly, out of the blue, emerged as an image of Napoleon on horseback. This brought a characteristic belly laugh from Don José Coronel, and soon we were in the jeep, jolting along on our way to the lake which surrounds Solentiname.

We got to the island late at night. Awaiting us were Teresa and William and a gringo poet, along with some other young men of the community. We went to bed almost immediately, but not before I'd caught sight of some paintings stacked in a corner. Ernesto was busy talking with his people and unpacking the various provisions and gifts he'd brought from San José. Someone was sleeping in a hammock. But once I'd seen those paintings, I had to go through them. They were so engrossing that I don't remember who it was that explained to me they were all works by the local campesinos. "Vicente did this one; this is Ramona's." Some were signed, others were not, but all were beautiful. Again and again the primal vision of the world, a world washed clear by the artist's eye, all the everyday surroundings seen as in a hymn of praise: miniature cows grazing in fields of poppies, a sugar-making hut with people swarming out of it like ants, a green-eyed horse against a sweep of cane, a baptism in a church which refused all perspective, seeming to clamber up and then slip back aslant, a lake with boats like tiny shoes, and, in the far distance, an enormous fish laughing with turquoise teeth.

Ernesto explained to me that the occasional sale of a painting helped the community make ends meet. In the morning, he promised, he would show me other works by the campesinos, their sculptures, and works in wood or stone. We were falling asleep on our feet, but I could not stop looking at those paintings piled high in that corner. Slowly I shuffled through the entire pack of stretched-canvas playing cards, with their tiny cows and flowers and that mother with two children on her knees, a white child and a red child, under a sky so studded with stars that the only cloud seemed to be huddling fearfully in a corner, as if trying to escape from the picture frame.

The next day was Sunday. Mass at eleven. The mass of Solentiname, during which the campesinos and Ernesto and some visiting friends would pick a passage from the New Testament to discuss. The theme that day was Jesus' arrest in the garden, a theme the people of Solentiname responded to with particular emotion, knowing its relevance to their own lives. They talked of the ever-present danger of the National Guard, which might sweep down on them at any moment, in the night or in broad daylight. They spoke of the constant fear which permeated life on the island, and on the mainland, and everywhere in Nicaragua, and not only in all of Nicaragua, but almost everywhere in Latin America—a life haunted by fear and by violent death: the life in Guatemala and El Salvador, in Argentina and in Bolivia, in Chile, Santo Domingo and Paraguay, in Brazil and in Colombia.

AFTER the mass, it was time to think about leaving the island. Remembering the canvases, I returned to the community center to look at them again in the full, delirious light of noon. The colors were intensified: acrylics and oils colliding in the form of miniature horses and sunflowers, fiestas in shining meadows and groves of symmetrical palms. Recalling I still had a roll of color film, I carried an armful of paintings out to the veranda, where Sergio, who was just coming in, held them up one by one for me in the brilliant light as I photographed them carefully, centering them in the viewfinder so that each painting would fill an entire frame. Such is chance: I had exactly as many exposures as there were paintings. I got them all. When Ernesto came to tell us the boat was ready, I told him what I'd done. "Thief of art," he chuckled, "smuggler of images!"

"That's right," I confessed, "I'm carting them all off, and I'll project them on my screen at home, and they'll be bigger and more dazzling than your originals," I grinned. "So sue me, *poeta!*"

Then the return to San José. From there I flew on to Havana, where I had a number of things to do before finally flying home to Paris. I arrived in Paris fatigued, a fatigue weighted with nostalgia. At Orly, a very quiet Claudine was awaiting me, and once again it was the life of wristwatches and committees, of *merci monsieur, bonjour madame,* the life of films, red wine and Claudine, of Mozart quartets and Claudine. But among the many things my suitcases spewed out over the bed and carpet, among the magazines and clippings and handkerchiefs and books by Central American poets, were the little gray plastic tubes containing rolls of film. How many things my camera had seen in the past two months—the Lenin School in Havana, the streets of Trinidad, the Irazú volcano, with its crater of hot green water, where Samuel and Sarita and I shared a vision of boiled ducks floating in sulfurous fumes.

Claudine took the rolls of film to be developed. One afternoon, walking through the Latin Quarter, I found the receipt in my pocket and hurried to pick them up—eight rolls—images suddenly returning of those paintings in Solentiname. Back in my apartment I checked the boxes to find the first slide in the Nicaragua series. I remembered that I had first shot Ernesto's mass, then children playing in palm groves exactly like those in the paintings, children and palm groves and cows against a violent blue sky and a lake only a bit more violently green, or was it the other way around? I put this box into the slide carrousel, knowing that the paintings would appear near the end of the roll.

By then it was dark. I was alone. After getting off work, Claudine would come to listen to music and stay with me. I put up the screen and poured out a rum with plenty of ice. Projector ready, carrousel loaded, remote control button in place, I settled back. No need to close the curtains. Night had conveniently darkened the room, lighting the streetlamps outside, releasing the hot perfume of rum. I felt glad it would all be coming back to me. First the paintings, then the Cuban slides. But why the paintings first? Why art before life? Why this professional distortion? But why not? said one voice to the other in that eternal dialogue, that bitter, fraternal argument. Why not look first at the paintings of Solentiname, if they too are life, since it's all the same?

The slides of the mass clicked rapidly by, poor images, underexposed. But the children came out well, their white teeth brilliant in the full light of the meadow. I almost hated to push the advance button, wanting to linger with each image of this fragile, tiny island, Solentiname, surrounded by water and—*police,* exactly like this boy was surrounded, this boy I was suddenly seeing, almost without realizing, I had pressed the button and there he was, clearly outlined in the middle distance, his face broad and smooth and full of astonished disbelief as his body collapsed slowly forward, a dark hole appearing in his forehead, the officer's pistol still indicating the trajectory of the bullet, and beside him there were others with submachine guns and a blurred background of houses and trees.

Think what you will, this is something which happens so fast you are left somewhere far, far behind. Blinking, I told myself they must have made some mistake at the developers, must have given me somebody else's slides. But here was the mass, the children playing in the meadow, so how—? My hand seemed to have a will of its own as it pushed the button: an endless field of salt glittering in the light of noon, a couple of shacks of rusted, corrugated metal, people crowding toward the left to stare at the corpses laid out on their backs, arms flung out, faces reflecting naked gray sky. Squinting, I could just make out a small group of men in uniforms in the background, moving away toward a jeep at the top of a hill.

I know I continued on, defying all sanity. I had no choice but to keep hitting that button, staring now at the intersection of Corrientes and San Martín in Buenos Aires, a black car with four guys aiming pistols at somebody running away in a white shirt and flapping slippers; then two women scrambling to take cover behind a parked truck; now a man looking straight at me in horrified disbelief, hand raised as if to touch his chin and feel himself still alive. Next, suddenly, a darkened room, a dim, dishwatery light seeping through a small, grilled window high on a wall, a naked girl on her back on a table, her hair hanging to the floor, a tall shadowy back jabbing a wire between her open legs while two guys in the foreground were talking off to one side, a blue necktie and a green sweater. I don't know if I was pushing the button or not, but a jungle clearing came into view, a hut with a thatched roof visible through foreground trees, and, against a tree trunk, a very thin young man looking off to his left toward a shifting group of five, maybe six figures crowded together, taking aim with rifles and pistols. Extremely thin, a distinct lock of hair on his dark forehead, one hand half-raised, the other perhaps in the pocket of his pants, he was looking right at the guns, as if calmly explaining something, as though he had all the time in the world. At that moment I knew, though the slide was out of focus, yes, I *knew* I was seeing Roque Dalton. Instantly I jabbed at the button, wanting somehow to save him from the outrage of his death. And now a car was exploding in sharp fragments in the populous heart of a city which might have been Buenos Aires or Sâo Paulo. Again the button, punching it fast, now volleys of bleeding faces and pieces of bodies, and women scrambling with children up a steep slope in Bolivia or Guatemala, and—suddenly the screen went blank, filling with the glow of white mercury and emptiness and Claudine, whose shadow was thrown on the screen as she came quietly in and leaned down to kiss me on the head and ask if the slides had come out well, if I was pleased with them, if I would show them to her.

I brought the carrousel back to the beginning. You never know how or why you've done a certain thing, gone beyond a certain limit you were unaware was even there until you'd crossed it. Without looking at Claudine, not wanting to alarm her with what must have been the look on my face, I got up and slowly sat her down in my chair. Maybe I said something about getting her a drink, or maybe I suggested she go ahead and start the slides while I mixed her a drink, I don't know. But I went into the bathroom, and I think I cried. Or maybe I threw up, or just wept, sitting there on the edge of the tub, letting time pass until I had the strength to go to the kitchen and mix Claudine her favorite drink, filling the glass with lots of ice, slowly becoming aware of the silence, realizing that Claudine was not crying out or rushing in to ask me what was happening—silence, only silence, and now and then the strains of a sugary *bolero* drifting in from the apartment next door. I don't know how long it took me finally to get from the kitchen to the living room to see the back of the screen just as Claudine neared the end of the slides, and white glare flooded the room. Claudine snapped off the projector and the room went dark. Smiling slowly at me, contented as a cat, she sank back in the chair to sip her drink.

"How nicely they came out," she said. "That one with the laughing fish, and the mother with the two kids and those little cows in the field. And wait, that one of the baptism in that country church! But you don't see any signatures. Who painted them?"

Sitting on the floor, I looked away from her. I picked up my glass and finished my drink. I wasn't going to tell her anything. What was there to say? But I remember I had an idiotic impulse to ask if anywhere in the slides she had seen a picture of Napoleon on horseback.

San José
Havana
April 1976

New Nicaragua

THIEVERY AND OTHER FINE THINGS

THOUGH I'm not entirely without imagination, if a month ago somebody had told me I'd be flying to Nicaragua aboard Somoza's jet I'd have answered, like a good citizen of Buenos Aires, "Go sing that tango to Gardel!"*

Nevertheless, I have to acknowledge that so far my entries into Nicaragua have not been exactly conventional. The first time, three years ago, I entered clandestinely in a small plane which took off from Costa Rica carrying Ernesto Cardenal, Sergio Ramírez, Oscar Castillo and myself to the frontier, where trusted friends transported us in jeeps and boats to Solentiname. But I've already told this story elsewhere, though at the time some may have thought they were reading fiction. In fact, I'm beginning to think that in things having to do with Nicaragua, the boundary between fiction and reality is a fluid one, at least where I'm concerned. Because this second trip—now the opposite of clandestine—also had dreamlike touches. Although it began as a waking nightmare: in the middle of downtown Panama City (where my *compañera* Carol and I had some time to spend before our flight to Managua) we were robbed by an expert who slipped away with almost everything we had, including our passports.

LOSING a passport is always a fearful thing, especially when the authorities of our countries may never give us another one, and when it's impossible to board a plane without papers, cards, stamps, counterstamps and canceled stamps. The nightmare turned decidedly Kafkaesque when we found ourselves in police headquarters—red tape being red tape—having to explain in minute detail an event which had happened in seconds. In situations like this I try to remove myself to a sort of higher ground, where I can look on with detachment (all in my head, of course), able to participate with all my reserves of good humor intact.

Looking up from his typewriter, the police official asked: "Dad's name?" while I'm wondering what in hell a man who's been dead for over thirty-five years has to do with all this. But I had to explain that his name was Julio, though for all it mattered I might have rebaptized him Hilario or Constantino.

The Kafkaesque nightmare (where everything is vaguely menacing and interminably and pointlessly drawn out, as if in our interrogation as robbery victims we might gradually be transformed into the suspects and finally into the perpetrators of some dire crime) abruptly shifted to something vastly preferable when an emissary of General Omar Torrijos* arrived upon the scene. General Torrijos, hearing of our presence in Panama, had sent out orders for us to be found. He then put all the detectives in the city on the track of the passport thief.

Though our passports never did materialize, what did was

this: tall drinks, icy and alcoholic and necessary, and an unforgettable hospitality, warm yet dignified, and most important of all, a conversation with Omar Torrijos, a man whose inner strength was hidden behind an easy cordiality. In Torrijos I sensed that same difficulty with making contact, that same shyness I have myself when I don't know someone well, a reserve which gradually gave way, ending in an openness which overwhelmed us both. If I had to sum up Torrijos' personality, I'd invoke the image of the leopard—that suave, effortless grace beneath which smolders an explosive power.

But the irrational was not finished with us yet. When reality intensifies beyond a certain point, it may suddenly change form, as in fairy tales and dreams, and anything may happen. Concerned with our immediate problem, Torrijos offered to send us to Managua in his private plane. We had just accepted that plan when one of his assistants entered with news from Nicaragua: Comandante Tomás Borge,* Minister of the Interior, had heard of our difficulties and had ordered a plane sent to bring us back in the morning to Managua. So there we were: after seeing ourselves deprived of all possibility of movement, suddenly two private planes were at our disposal. Torrijos amiably withdrew his offer, arranging for us to be taken to the military airport in the morning. But what comes next merits a separate paragraph.

A FREE SKY

STREAMLINED, gleaming, with two young pilots and a stewardess on her maiden flight and just as excited as we were: Somoza's jet, left behind in the sudden departure of the tyrant and his cohorts. In the cabin of the plane were two huge chairs with a table between and a lateral bench to seat four, everything slathered with animal pelts and stinking of dollars. The height of symbolism was the bathroom, where you had to look very carefully to find the necessary convenience, since that, as well as the walls and the floor, was hidden under sumptuous hangings, like the tent of an Arab sheik in a Hollywood film.

Flying to Managua in such an astonishing airplane went far beyond the dreamlike, and we savored every minute, along with a couple of sandwiches and cups of black coffee. Having settled into a spacious chair, I tried to imagine the conversations between the dictator and his cronies, his buzzard eyes looking out the tiny windows over the fields and crops—his own personal fiefdom, the incontestable realm of the dynasty. I imagined his usual reception at the airport, the National Guard in formation, the snap of servile salutes, so different from the joyous improvisation of young revolutionaries which greeted our arrival. As we taxied up to an empty hangar, our friends and the journalists were waiting for us on the exact opposite side of the airfield, a problem soon remedied by a car, which brought us together in a few minutes. For the second time I was bathed in Nicaragua, a second beautiful immersion in the fluid life of a people overwhelmed with the joy of liberation and rebirth. Radio spots, TV appearances, lightning interviews—all in the midst of embraces and places and news and contradictions and the first glimpses of the armed militia, boys and girls with submachine guns and pistols and sometimes indescribable uniforms, and always, invariably, the smile of liberty, which also means the liberty to smile.

Tomás Borge had not only sent a plane, but invited us to stay in his house with him and his wife Josephine. And Ernesto Cardenal was awaiting us in the Ministry of Culture, ready to thrust an itinerary under my nose (which I fought like a tiger to reduce to human proportions). I'm glad things worked out this way because, out of the friendly rivalry of two ministries, not to mention a third (that of Sergio Ramírez), a week emerged in which I not only had cultural engagements but close contact with workers in the cities and in the countryside. Canceling a couple of panel discussions, I took part instead in several mass meetings in the provinces. It wasn't easy sometimes, because affection and friendship have a way of requiring of one the gift of being everywhere at once. But a week was enough, I think, to take in the broad outlines of this enclave of hope which Nicaragua now is for all Latin America.

My memories are not systematic. I can only touch upon the wealth of things I've seen and learned, but many others— historians, sociologists and journalists—will be covering this same ground in depth, so that eventually the revolution of the Nicaraguan people will be better known and receive the support and cooperation it so greatly needs and deserves.

CROSSROADS OF CHILDREN

THE term *revolution* is used in Nicaragua to designate the state of affairs following the triumph of the Sandinista Front for National Liberation, after the infamous decades of Somoza. Technically that term is correct only if used in reference to a future project, while the term *liberation* corresponds entirely to the present reality.

For obvious reasons the new government has had to initiate changes with a caution already under attack by more radical groups, but which the vast majority of the people understands and supports. Only with such mass support has it been possible to accomplish so much in so little time. The transformation in four short months has been astounding—lines of force accelerating in all directions to rebuild from the ground up a country devastated by plunder, by terror and by the monstrous unleashing of the National Guard in the final stages of the fighting.

A telling symbol: entering a classroom at the Central American University (UCA) in Managua, I saw a blackboard crowded with names of volunteers for the literacy campaign which will begin in March 1980. A recent census, as thorough as possible under the circumstances, has brought to light the disastrous neglect of education under Somoza. Teachers and students are now drawing up plans, putting together teams, and allocating resources for the literacy effort. Whenever literacy is mentioned in a mass meeting, I can see the tremendous enthusiasm this program is going to generate throughout the country. On the eve of our departure, the first contingent of one hundred Cuban teachers, experts in literacy, arrived in Nicaragua. Their task will be to orient their Nicaraguan colleagues, especially the high school and university students. It's worth noting that right now in Cuba one thousand Nicaraguan children (three hundred of whom actually fought with the Sandinistas) are studying with Cuban children on the "Isle of Youth."

The members of the leadership have a very good sense of the problems involved in readapting so many children and young people to their natural condition as minors and stu-

dents. You have only to go into the streets to see the smooth
faces of young boys, armed and in uniform, carrying out their
militia duties with an evident sense of exercising a well-
earned right. Young girls barely at the age of puberty stand
guard with heavy submachine guns. More than once boys and
girls were pointed out to us—some very young—who as guerrilla soldiers had fought ferociously against the National
Guard. One afternoon at the seashore with Sergio Ramírez
and Tomás Borge a boy of about fifteen whose name now slips
my mind was warmly greeted and welcomed into our circle.
As a guerrilla fighter of outstanding courage and marksman-
ship, he had brought down thirty Guardsmen. Now he was
licking an ice cream cone, smiling, and answering the questions of Tomás and Sergio. It wasn't easy to imagine him back
in school, and his case is only one of many throughout the
country. On one hand, a vast number of illiterates; on the
other, a generation between childhood and adolescence which
has lived the drama of adults and which today, in conditions
that finally are normal, will have real problems adjusting to
that normalcy.

AGAIN THE CHILDREN

A compañero named David was in charge of our security,
which was extensive, but appropriate given the situation in
the country at that time. The clemency of the Sandinistas at
the end of the fighting was almost unbelievable. The decision
by the national leadership *not* to send large numbers of
Guardsmen to the firing squad—Guardsmen who had committed atrocities right up through the final moments of bat-

tle—had been a positive thing in that the people generally approved of this clemency, preferring to turn immediately to the future rather than to adjust the dark accounts of the past. But the Somocista forces have regrouped and here and there under cover of night are carrying out ambushes, disturbing the peace and creating alerts which could well upset people who remained on the sidelines during the battle for liberation.

At dawn on our third day in Managua, we heard gunfire in the neighborhood of Tomás Borge's house. In the morning, we were told it was only a bunch of drunks; some guys with guns shooting at the stars to pass the time. But we didn't believe it, since the gunfire had been coming from different directions, slowing converging upon Borge's house. No doubt it will be some time before the country will be free of roving gunmen who harbor the insane hope of changing a reality which so clearly has the support of the immense majority. In any case, foreigners are especially well guarded, and all around me I was impressed with the discipline of the young militiamen, who wouldn't let even one of their *compañeros* enter certain areas with their weapons, letting them pass only after verifying their identity and their business. One grows accustomed to going about in the midst of pistols and machine guns: back in Caracas it seemed strange not to see arms in the airport and on the streets; it seemed odd to ride in a car without an enormous submachine gun on somebody's lap or leaning against a window.

David, a refined and well-educated *compañero,* was also much more interested in talking about the future than about the past (only once, on a trip to León where he had fought, did he tell us the story of some episode in the war). But he could not get over being amazed at what was happening in the country (almost as amazed as we were). We were moved to see how elated he was at the spectacle of life in the streets, the bustling schools, the open shops, but he was especially thrilled to see the children, their laughing, boisterous presence, their voices and games everywhere, where only four months earlier death had prowled, dressed in the uniform of the National Guard.

"Nobody let them play outdoors," David told us. "Because the Guard would kill them, just for the fun of it, to terrify the people in a neighborhood. And the Guard knew that plenty of these kids could fight just as well as anybody, so they feared them and hated their guts. If a kid climbed up a tree to get a piece of fruit or to look off into the distance, a Guardsmen might pick him off, just for the hell of it, to see him fall. But now . . ."

Now there's an incredible amount to see. Managua and the rest of the country are swarming with young people. At mass demonstrations, you see kids clambering up the same trees which before might have cost them their lives. Peering out over the crowds in the squares, they look like little monkeys or tropical flowers among the treetops. When high school lets out, groups of teenagers flag down trucks and cars, which pick them up and drop them off nearer their houses. The very poorest have gone back to their jobs—shining shoes, hawking newspapers on busy intersections, hanging around restaurants asking for change. I don't know the official policy on population growth, but I can say that many more schools, cafeterias and health clinics will be needed, as well as more textbooks and vaccines (a nationwide campaign of polio vaccination is now being planned, which will cost far more than what the state can pay at this time).

Inevitably, my thoughts return to almost twenty years ago,

and I see myself on my first trip to Cuba, that great initial example of Latin American revolution. I see the same things—the literacy campaign like a hurricane of laughter and blackboards all over the island. I see schools springing up like mushrooms, and health centers and playgrounds. I hear Fidel talking about the children as now I hear Ernesto Cardenal and the Minister of Health and Comandante Borge and all those who are looking ahead and who know that somewhere in the distance a child is waiting and trusting.

SHOWING THE WAY

THE poet Cardenal (most call him *padre*) still wears his ever-present beret and white shirt. The same Cardenal who brought me secretly by boat to Solentiname now receives me in his office in the Ministry of Culture. Here people are coming and going, agreeing and disagreeing, amid books and files and workers battling with phones, as well as with projects, meetings, conferences, panels, books to be published—and with very little money to do it all.

The office of Sergio Ramírez was emptier, almost austere, perhaps because Sergio wasn't there much, but traveling all over to announce new measures, to confer with the population, to swear in regional members of the government (in Siuna three women were given these posts in a population of miners, a good sign in a country where machismo is not exactly a thing of the past). I didn't see the office of Tomás Borge, one of the most famous heroes of the armed struggle and now Minister of the Interior, but staying in his house I sometimes had the impression that Tomás was running his

Ministry out of there. Perhaps not, but I don't think I'm entirely mistaken.

I've known Cardenal and Sergio Ramírez for years, but to get to know and to form a friendship with Tomás Borge has been one of the highest rewards of this first trip to Nicaragua after the victory. I'm sure I'll be back soon, for if elephants are contagious (as the Surrealists said), Cuba and Nicaragua for me are even more so, and there's no antidote for this ailment. Nor do I want to be cured. To know Borge as a political leader and as a man has been one of those experiences words cannot relate. Better silence and allusion.

In Tomás Borge I see a man of poetic sensibility living in times which oblige him to be a political leader. His handshake conveys an iron will that is nonetheless incapable of causing pain. I had read his memoir of Carlos Fonseca,* founder (with other heroes) of the Sandinista Front, which organized the grass-roots movement that overthrew Somoza. In that brief text, written in prison, Tomás revealed his own personality without ever putting himself in the foreground. He stands back on those pages, alluding to himself only as "being possessed by the god of wrath and by the demon of tenderness." He alone could have described in so few words the admirable personality of Carlos Fonseca, and at the same time, without realizing it, described himself, sketching himself in the background, and in a modest, completely unrhetorical style. Almost everything is said without directly saying it (revolutionary writers, please take note: Borge's book is a rare example of revolutionary style, totally without the clichés we so often hear in books and speeches).

Deep, tender friend, now and forever, I know that at some point out of my hearing, you said to Carol, "Take care of

Julio, take good care of him." Of course she will take care of me, but you are the one, Tomás, who must take care, because your people need you, as they need all your *compañeros.* I'll say no more. More words aren't needed between us. Your life is with Nicaragua, and your people are today the most vital in the world, the most beautiful and the most free.

WHERE IS THE SOLIDARITY WITH NICARAGUA?

SOMETIMES when the leaders here speak of solidarity, it is with a wry, slightly bitter smile. Let's not mince words. International solidarity has not been generous with Nicaragua. The whole world is now aware of what the war of liberation has cost, a war in which the Somocistas did not hesitate to carry out the sadistic bombing of Nicaragua's major cities. Everybody knows the war meant the abandonment of crops, the destruction of livestock, the paralysis of small industries and manufacturing enterprises and the further deterioration of conditions which under the boot of Somoza were already miserable.

Does this not call for the immediate donation of equipment, technical assistance, books and medicines by countries which have often responded favorably to comparatively less serious situations? The Nicaraguans are not asking for anything. They maintain the proud silence of people who have won a battle on their own and who are prepared to fight on without help. But foreigners who visit the country—and are hit in the face with the overwhelming needs of the Nicaraguan people—have a duty to ask on their behalf, to be spontaneous spokesmen for a country which in the coming months will find itself facing a drastic shortage of food products (including milk for children) which cannot be purchased without foreign exchange. To help Nicaragua today is to help the cause of freedom and justice in Latin America. Is that perhaps why so little aid has been forthcoming, oh pseudo-democracies of this world . . . ?

Barely liberated itself, the tiny Caribbean island of Grenada, with one of the poorest populations in the world, collected five thousand dollars for Nicaragua, a sum which represented, proportionally, a greater compassion than the contributions from the United States. The Nicas will never forget that. There's an apocryphal story going around about Chile sending a grand total of two boxes of canned milk, a carton of medicine, and seventy mattresses. A smear, no doubt, against the reputation of General Pinochet, who is—as he says himself—a man who is often smeared. But I think of the two hundred Cuban doctors who are working at this very moment throughout the country. I've already mentioned the contingent of one hundred Cuban literacy teachers. As far as I know, Cuba has no surplus of doctors, quite the contrary. But true cooperation is not a question of *surplus,* but of brotherhood, and as almost always happens, the poor countries are the best brothers to other poor countries in trouble.

Though I don't have exact figures, the aid for Nicaragua was much greater at the time of the earthquake which leveled Managua in 1972. As everyone now knows, Somoza and his shrewd collaborators took that opportunity to siphon off for themselves the lion's share of the aid sent for the population. Which is why Managua is still a city in ruins. It's sadly ironic to think that now, when the aid would go directly into the hands of an entire people deeply committed to rebuilding their economy and to ımproving the health and education of their children, this aid should be stinted or denied.

But let's not be totally pessimistic at the end of these reflections so full of light and hope. Among my international readers there may be some Minister of Finance or of Agriculture or of Health, or the president of a foundation, or of a banking consortium who is capable of understanding this harsh reality and of organizing plans for action. The Nicaraguans won't ask for anything, but they can't prevent me from asking for them, and I do it out of admiration and love for the courage I see and for the lesson they are giving to our bitter and suffering Latin America.

A Sovereign People

S*EVERAL* months after the ousting of Somoza, Nicaragua kicked off a nationwide literacy campaign. For the foreseeable future the whole country will be an immense school where, somehow, one half of the population will teach the other half to read and write.

Only once before has Latin America witnessed such a dramatic and emotional mobilization, with the goal of a real awakening of consciousness. Shortly after the overthrow of Batista in 1959, the Cuban people became both actor and audience in a titanic effort to wrest themselves out of ignorance and underdevelopment. Their success has prompted the Nicaraguans to try to repeat it, and if possible to go beyond it. Two small Latin American countries are showing the way which one day many other countries will also have to follow on a continent where illiteracy is not only a massive obstacle to progress and development but a crushing negative factor in the search for roots, that search for an authentic identity which in different and confused ways can be seen in the recent history of Latin America.

In a curious irony, the independence movements which

gave birth to our countries had a shared vision of mass education and culture, an ideal which their heroes and progenitors inherited from the French Revolution. Under the banner of Romanticism these ideals were put forward in proclamations, constitutions and governmental acts. The notion of "educating the sovereign" was commonly held in the nineteenth century, the belief that only a man who could read and write was capable of being a good citizen. But almost immediately civil wars broke out. The emergence of *caudillos* and their ensuing dictatorships and increasingly arrogant tyrannies put an emphatic end to democratic dreams and plans which only very gradually and under vastly more favorable conditions might have been realized. Latin America's vast geography, its ethnic differences, the periodic invasions by foreign powers (in collusion with local despots)—all combined to isolate and alienate our peoples. Docile, ignorant masses were preferred, not citizens capable of learning, thinking, and criticizing. Nicaragua is an extreme example of how forty years of oppression and exploitation translate directly into a burden of illiteracy estimated at more than 60 percent of the population.

The liberation of the Nicaraguan people on July 19, 1979, was immediately manifest in a will to *reconstruct* which went far beyond the material sense of that word. When the national leadership calls itself a government of reconstruction, it uses that term knowing it is fully understood by those who have experienced the bitter costs of ignorance in their own flesh and blood. It's no surprise that accomplished poets and intellectuals such as Ernesto Cardenal, Sergio Ramírez and Tomás Borge are members of this government. For them, reconstruction means not simply raising the country out of smoking ruins but raising all the children and all the adults to a level of full participation—conscious, critical participation—in the work ahead. Speak with any of these leaders and you'll see how their sense of reconstruction begins with the idea of the Nicaraguan citizen as an active worker in this process, fully capable of understanding the job to be done, why it is necessary, and how it ought to be carried out. The devastating notion of a passive people, brutally enforced by Somoza, has shifted to a nationwide dynamic of participation and consultation, a process unimaginable without a minimum of intellectual preparation. This preparation involves the reassessment of atavistic and traditional beliefs, making use of them when they seem positive, or leaving them definitively behind when they contribute to regression and stagnation.

All this should make it easy to understand the intense energy now pouring into the literacy campaign in Nicaragua. Since even the most elementary tools were lacking, from pencils to textbooks, it was obvious to the entire population that the campaign could not advance without the aid which would have to come from friendly nations. In this connection, I should point out that UNESCO's call for funds was a wholehearted response to Nicaragua's decision, in the face of which indifference or hesitation are impossible. However, in the 1960s in Cuba it was another story entirely. At that time UNESCO sat back, awaiting the outcome of the campaign, stepping in only to verify the results and announce them with enthusiastic praise. Now UNESCO is no longer hesitating but calling out for worldwide assistance, thus demonstrating its full confidence that one more Latin American country will have the strength to emerge from underdevelopment.

Official reports estimate that Somoza's barbaric genocide— including the indiscriminate bombing of cities and rural towns—represents a loss to Nicaraguan education of more than 100 million córdobas (around $10 million) in destroyed school buildings, school furniture and educational equipment and materials. This destruction, along with the ghastly totals of thirty thousand dead and nearly one hundred thousand wounded, indicates the full measure of difficulties which must be faced in this next battle, the battle for mass education. The problems are numerous: shortage of materials, insufficient transportation, insufficient funds, the difficulties of communicating with the undeveloped zones of the interior (especially with the Atlantic coast) plus the need to carry the campaign to regions of predominantly Indian populations (Miskitos, Sumos, etc.). How are all these problems to be solved?

The solution is a practical one: anyone who can read and write should join the campaign and teach literacy. High school students, not yet employed and hence able to devote all their energies to the task, will provide the greater part of the workforce. Brigade members, who must be at least thirteen years old, will be sent to both urban and rural areas. Accompanied by more experienced advisors and with all the necessary logistics, they will be sent to live in fields and forests, in factories, in mountain villages and in urban ports. They will share the homes as well as the work of their students, most of whom will be adults. The entire country will become a single school, and the teaching methods will be developed in the course of the work. The Indian population, with their deeply rooted native cultures, will be taught in Indian languages as well as in Spanish. On the Atlantic coast, English is also spoken, which presents another problem to be solved.

The adult literacy drive is absolutely essential, but a visit to more remote parts of the country, or to any city, will reveal that both the government and the citizenry have given their maximum attention and concern to the children. With the country's liberation, the young people have been thrust into a drastically changed life, and in a very few years the responsibility of carrying this process forward will fall to them. The fact that young people make up the great bulk of the army of literacy workers only serves to emphasize further this dual aspect, which gives the literacy campaign its unique and unmistakable quality.

Nicaraguan families have not ceased to marvel at the incredible change, a change you can breathe in the streets, in the public squares, in all public places—a change which means freedom and safety. Perhaps the loveliest, most touching symbol of this change is the visible ebullience of the children, their excited games and songs.

In my first exploration of Managua, I was astonished to see my companions, young Sandinista soldiers, react with almost delirious enthusiasm whenever they saw children out in the streets. Under Somoza, they finally explained, children didn't play in the streets, because the National Guard suspected them of revolutionary activities, or they simply detested them on general principle, knowing that many of these kids were Sandinista couriers and quite capable of taking part in military actions. So the Guard would often arrest and kill one of these kids in order to terrorize the population.

"The mere appearance of a uniform scattered kids like sparrows," one of my companions told me. "The Guard even outlawed kickball in the vacant lots—convinced it was a cover for military training."

When children see soldiers today, that uniform is their

guarantee of protection and friendship. I saw this over and over again as kids crowded around us, fascinated (not surprisingly) by the pistols and submachine guns of the young soldiers.

But the participation of young people in the literacy campaign has presented problems not so readily solved. First, there is the risk. Many of these young people would be in danger in regions far removed from the cities, regions where the Somocistas, who have taken refuge in neighboring countries or who are hiding out in Nicaragua, have made no secret of their plans to seek revenge. In Cuba, it was remembered, some young volunteers had actually been killed by counter-revolutionaries operating out of the Escambray Mountains.

Weighing these risks, the Sandinista leadership determined that only those youths properly authorized by their parents would be permitted to travel to the more perilous zones, which is, naturally, where most of them wanted to go. In Managua I was able to follow some of these developments, which were often quite dramatic. Some parents refused to sign the authorizations, a painful frustration for their children, particularly for those whose classmates had permission to go.

The young people took matters into their own hands in a way which might seem surprising if you haven't recently spent time with the Nicaraguan people. The children who had permission not only encouraged those whose parents had refused, but they formed commissions and went to visit the parents, asking them to reconsider and grant the permission their children desired.

And in all of this there was nothing in the least compulsory. It now seems clear that the great majority of high school students will leave in March, along with a large number of teachers and university students, to work on a project which will exalt them and fill them with pride. Each student will carry a packet of literacy materials, prepared in Nicaragua and printed in Costa Rica—a meager baggage with which to confront inexperience, the uncertainties of climate, the hazards of geography, endemic illness, food shortages, and the harshness of life in regions which are often inhospitable.

All this, I think, should make it easier to understand UNESCO's urgent plea on behalf of Nicaraguan literacy. An estimated $20 million is needed, a modest sum compared with the huge budgets for war and with the bloated size of commercial profits. Yet it would be enough to help this nation of fewer than three million people hoist themselves once and for all out of backwardness. The Somoza regime, which prolonged this state of affairs, scurried out of the country with a lot more than that in its pockets.

Nicaraguan Sketches

PENCIL DRAWINGS, NOT PHOTOGRAPHS

I'M writing these lines for those who know Nicaragua only through the mass media. Rough drafts, rapidfire sketches: they are meant to bring the reader a bit nearer to the air breathed in that country, to what people are saying and doing in their daily lives. I want the reader to see through my eyes, to plunge with me into the streets, to glimpse life along the country roads, to experience a little of the incredible freshness of Nicaragua today.

Reporters usually skip such things. concerned with more serious matters, but on my very first drive through Managua, after two years' absence, I came across the perfect symbol of just how much the country has evolved in two years. Back then I'd explored those neighborhoods in the eastern part of the city known as the Oriental barrios, perhaps the poorest in that entire poverty-smashed capital. I'd gone on foot then, since neither buses nor taxis could get through without bogging down in streets which were nothing but gullies of mud. Yet now, I suddenly realized, our car was moving right through those barrios, as the *compañero* at the wheel pointed out the new busstops, plazas and sparkling new asphalt pavements.

"They did this in record time," he explained. "Now everybody comes and goes with no problem."

"But all this paving! So many kilometers," I said, amazed.

"That's right," he said. "The people here got going. Everybody took up a shovel."

Where two years earlier pigs were snuffling in vile ooze, now buses were speeding through, crammed with students and workers. I remember having seen shacks and yards as filthy and rundown as any I'd seen. Now I could hardly recognize the neighborhood. Everything was clean and freshly painted. Big terracotta pots of flowers lined bright sidewalks. What a cheerful, convivial feeling!

"The people did it all," said the *compañero,* as if that were the most natural thing in the world.

Two hours later, as the day drew to a close, we heard on the radio that Somocista bands had just blown up a dam and several bridges. So the scale tipped, as that too was thrust into the more than symbolic balance of Nicaragua's painful day-to-day reality.

Yes, an immensity of change has occurred here in two years. The differences are unmistakably evident. Nobody's been wasting time here, for good or for ill. This nation which finally overthrew Somoza, after so many years and so many sacrificed lives, continues to respond almost unanimously to the directives of their new leadership.

But before I speak further of their dazzling achievements, I must mention that the opponents (potential and declared) of the new government have also been very active, looking for every possible way to wrench the country back to its previous condition. They have two identifiable strategies. One is to wrap themselves tightly in the flag of liberal democracy, which is neither liberal nor democratic, since their sole objective is to recover all the power and privileges that once belonged to the big landowners and to the proprietors of huge commercial and industrial enterprises. The other strategy is visible along the Honduran border and in the United States, where remnants of Somoza's National Guard are regrouping, eager to do anything at all to reconquer their lost land and to avenge themselves on the population which booted them out. On the flimsiest pretext they violate frontiers, committing random assaults, theft and violent sabotage. They openly murder both unarmed campesinos and militia fighters. This has gone so far that even as I write I hear on the radio that the Nicaraguan government has decided to recall its ambassador from Honduras, since all diplomatic protest has proved useless.

The persistent danger of invasion has made it necessary for Nicaragua to divert increasing amounts of its all-too-finite resources to defense, resources already precarious in such a small, underdeveloped country. When you consider that the militia force is nothing other than the civilian population armed and rapidly trained, you can easily understand why the work force has necessarily been diminished, just when the country was beginning to show signs of recovery, after the difficult time at the end of the war. The meager sums which under normal conditions would have gone to agriculture, housing, education or the improvement of living standards have had to be reduced in order to pay for defense. People are working with rifles near to hand, which is nothing new—they did this when the enemy was the government itself—the right to liberty and peace goes on being purchased with a brutal expenditure of time and vigilance, in a state of permanent alert.

If you come to Managua, be sure to visit the Museum of the Armed Forces, which is not some military mausoleum but a graphic chronicle of an epic battle against oppression. Deprived of liberty by foreign and domestic enemies, Nicaragua won independence only after intense suffering and prolonged sacrifice. Which, in the history of nations, is nothing new. Practically every country in the world has its historical museum where the stages of its struggles are retraced. But Nicaragua's museum is different from the others in spirit and in message. Like so many things in this remarkable country, it reveals a mentality, a *sensibility*, which until now I've never met with anywhere.

Starting with the landing of the U.S. Marines at the end of the nineteenth century, continuing through the interminable course of the Somoza tyranny, father and son (not to mention a nephew dreaming of revenge in Honduras, arming his mercenaries with the support of the United States), the museum traces the slow, arduous and sometimes astonishing progress of a people, virtually unarmed, who took on a powerful and implacable enemy.

While the figure of Augusto César Sandino* dominates the scene, the museum organizers have steered clear of all facile sentimentalism, all demagogic propaganda. Once again, a serene and dignified confidence is confirmed; these are people who know their own truth and have no need to reiterate it in deafening slogans. The halls of this modest museum succeed one another like separate moments in a good, clear lesson in history, with documents, maps, photos and the artifacts of war.

When you come to the final stages of the struggle, you would expect to see documentary evidence of the bloody Somoza horror: murders, tortures, the ravages inflicted by the National Guard. *There is none of that.* Instead, the faces of patriots fallen in combat or massacred in prison look out at us calmly from family photos, from snapshots with friends, from pictures taken in jungle or mountain camps. Humor is present, too: a uniform of Somoza plastered from neck to pants cuff with all the military decorations he left behind. An entire wall is devoted to the arms of the revolutionary fighters, rusty rifles going back to Sandino's day, others pieced together out of scraps, weapons nearly useless when you think of the tanks and the machine guns they opposed. Speaking of tanks, more humor: the tank given by Benito Mussolini to the elder Somoza is so small that people burst out laughing when they see it. I imagined myself having to drive this thing and asked them to take my picture beside it, hoping to preserve one of the more ludicrous memories of my life.

This time I had come to Managua to participate in the deliberations of the Committee of Intellectuals, formed in Havana in late 1981. One of our most urgent tasks was to put forward in Nicaragua what we had talked about in Cuba: the necessity of establishing amicable relations with intellectuals and with other groups in the United States (where more and more people are waking up to the arbitrary treatment of Nicaragua by the Reagan government). Coming over in the plane I had time to ask myself how our proposal might be received in Nicaragua. Would it go against the grain of the justifiable hostility the United States provokes in Central America? Would people be resentful, especially here, where Sandino fought for so many years against those same forces which persist in considering these countries as their backyard?

But this was to underestimate the clear distinction that even the simplest Nicaraguan makes between the government in Washington and the people of the United States. At the very first session of the committee I realized our proposal would be well received. Cuba's Minister of Culture, Armando Hart, did not mince words about the urgency of taking our message straight to the intellectuals and honest citizens of the United States. Sergio Ramírez, speaking for the national leadership, affirmed their willingness to open this crucial dialogue. Later, talking to people in the streets, I found no opposition whatsoever based upon historical resentments. The Nicaraguan, with his own particular sensitivity, realizes that many people in the United States understand the Sandinista struggle, as well as the struggle in El Salvador, and that every day the opposition to Reagan's policy is gaining strength.

With this in mind, the members of our committee were spurred to organize the next step, a meeting next September in Mexico, which will bring together a large number of U.S. and Latin American artists and intellectuals. While such a meeting does not seem an unusual occurrence in Paris or in Mexico City, that it should also seem quite normal in Nicaragua seems to me extraordinary and very admirable, especially when you consider that people in Nicaragua are braced to fight to the death against any attempt to carry out the bellicose threats of Reagan and his advisors.

Between committee sessions I returned to the streets, in search of that daily reality which is the underpinning of everything, without which the most brilliant speeches are only words. I could see it immediately: many more consumer goods were available than two years ago, and at cheaper prices. The street markets were giving way to shopping centers where buyer and seller could meet in clean, spacious surroundings, in attractive, well-designed buildings. As in so many places where people congregate, the atmosphere is cheerful, with a nonstop flow of talking and joking about anything at all. What a contrast to the chill atmosphere in those exclusive centers where commerce has established its most pretentious and expensive boutiques. There, opposition is thick in the air, the resistance to change of people still thinking in individualist terms. These same attitudes fill the columns of the newspaper *La Prensa*, which takes advantage of its freedom to complain on a daily basis about every restriction which interferes with the interests of property owners and businessmen determined to preserve their privileges.

Reading the articles in *La Prensa*, where everything which isn't "democratic" (according to their definition) is automatically "Marxist," I can only admire the decision of the leaders to let the internal opposition express itself freely in this public forum. If the state of emergency (decreed under threat of imminent invasion) leads to a crackdown on this abuse of freedom of the press *(La Prensa)*, nobody will be able to attribute this to an authoritarian will to muzzle criticism. Yet for me the real pulse and truth of the situation is to be found, not in newspapers but in the streets, where you can see how people react to the selfishness of a minority which is still scrambling to salvage whatever scraps it can from the Somocista banquet. The existence of cheerful, pleasant shopping centers is a direct symbol of the attitude of the masses, a direct challenge to a mentality which lingers on, still visible in so many private homes, restaurants and boutiques.

The reader may be familiar with the situation of the Miskito Indians, that substantial minority whose traditional homeland is in the Atlantic region of the country, separated by tradition, language and history from the Pacific zone, where the liberation of the country was started and brought to fruition. General Alexander Haig made a fool of himself a few months back when he presented a photograph of a pile of burning corpses, claiming it showed Sandinista militiamen destroying evidence—the bodies of Miskito Indians they had massacred. No less a paper than the left-wing *Le Figaro* of Paris ran this photo, quickly discredited by documentary evidence, as well as by a disclaimer from Haig himself. Nevertheless, such outrageous lies have led to an insistence that the government has herded the Miskitos into camps in order to control them, their loyalty to the revolution being in doubt.

If you get to Managua, it's worth making the trip to the Atlantic coast, accessible at last, thanks to the feat of a new highway, built in an incredibly short time. When you reach that coast, you will see that the Indians don't wear feathers but are very much like you and me, though they speak a different language and observe their traditional customs. Somoza's neglect of the Miskitos contributed to their remoteness from modern history, into which they are now being incorporated, thanks to the ongoing contacts recently established between the Sandinista leaders and the people of the Atlantic zone. The resettlement of the Miskitos was necessary, since their homelands on the Honduran frontier were at the mercy of Somocista bands, and they were also being subjected to virulent anti-Sandinista propaganda. The government is now providing the Miskitos with housing and lands in a secure area, as well as guaranteeing them the preservation of their customs and way of life, including their religion which, paradoxically, is the Protestantism taught by Moravian missionaries, who still retain all their traditional prestige. The problem of the Miskito Indians has been perhaps the most delicate and the most difficult the Sandinistas have had to face in a task which consists of almost nothing but serious problems.

I'm familiar with the indignant outrage which flares up in any given country at the least act of aggression against its interests or integrity. This sort of incident is often unscrupulously provoked or manipulated by regimes which seek to exploit real patriotic feeling. This is happening right now in Great Britain and Argentina around the issue of the Malvinas Islands.

Perhaps that's why I'm so continually astounded at how in Nicaragua the most tested courage and the most unshakable determination go hand in hand with a calm, a good humor and a courtesy which must have struck more than one journalist or European visitor as extremely strange.

Arriving in Managua, I heard talk everywhere about the so-called Central American Democratic Community, that laughable alliance of Costa Rica, Honduras and El Salvador which deliberately excludes Cuba and Nicaragua. This coalition, manipulated from the outset by the United States, is obviously meant to exert military and psychological pressure on Nicaragua through her closest neighbors. A similar encirclement would most likely have unleashed hysteria in any other country, but the Nicaraguans took it in stride, with what might seem like fatalistic acceptance, but which isn't that at all. There's absolutely nothing fatalistic about their determination to proceed despite this sort of machination (to which may be added direct U.S. threats and the daily menace of a counterrevolutionary invasion).

My conversation with various top-level Sandinista leaders—Tomás Borge, Sergio Ramírez and Miguel D'Escoto* among others—always leaves me with the impression of a serene lucidity in the face of danger, a danger which in no way diminishes their conviction that the Nicaraguan historical process will advance—no matter what. If this seems surprising, how much more amazing to see exactly the same attitude in the population at large.

I couldn't help being reminded of my last trip, when I attended the trials of several Somocista war criminals. I was astonished at the atmosphere of calm and objectivity, at the desire for justice, not vengeance, which reigned not only among the members of the tribunal but among the public in attendance. I'll never forget the trial of a particular colonel, where an overwhelming amount of evidence had been presented to the effect that, among other crimes and atrocities, he had ordered campesinos to be thrown out of helicopters above their native villages, in order to terrorize the population. Faced with these accusations, the colonel cynically denied the charges, maintaining that, in fact, he had done a number of good works in the countryside, inspired by a sense of Christian charity. Whereas in other countries public rage would have been impossible to control, in Managua this man was heard out in silence, in the certainty that justice would be done. The death sentence is now abolished in Nicaragua, despite so many unspeakable crimes. This fact alone is a barometer of a way of being which radically distinguishes the authentic Nicaraguan people from those who were their torturers and executioners.

Europeans, I think, are already familiar with the 1980 literacy campaign, which, according to statistical reports, has lowered the rate of illiteracy from over 50 percent to 11 percent. One half of the population did indeed teach the other half to read.

But as UNESCO and the specialists know, the real problems begin when the initial campaign is over. The task is then to maintain the ground won and little by little to create the habit of reading in people who—because of their isolation and the demands of work—tend to forget what they have learned. Nor have the Nicas been asleep in this area. After a period of planning and preparing materials, the CEP (Collective for Popular Education), made up of small groups of teachers and students, launched a new campaign this April. Some one hundred eighty thousand students and twenty-six thousand teachers will be involved.

Once again brigades of intellectuals, teachers, high school and university students will fan out over the whole country in an attempt to raise the general level of education in the population. Though the quality of radio programming is generally low in Latin America, in Nicaragua an entire program is devoted to the tasks of literacy. Progress has also been made in higher education.

But I think the most significant advance in this field has been the founding of the publishing house Nueva Nicaragua. In practically no time at all it has produced a series of paperbacks which are widely disseminated throughout the country. Also in preparation is a series of one hundred titles which will make available in cheap editions the great works of world literature. At a recent book fair, people snapped up a collection of five books packaged in an attractive little cardboard box, and at a price which would be a dream for French readers. The number of weeklies devoted to culture has also increased, one of which is *Ventana,* notable for its wide circulation as the weekly supplement of the daily paper, *Barricada.* This supplement is packed with fine literary work, as well as visual art, with reproductions of paintings and excellent critical essays.

The lively interest in culture is reflected in the eager attendances at cultural events; people don't attend these events out of duty or to pass the time, but in search of direct dialogue with poets, storytellers, visual artists and musicians. Gabriel García Márquez, Rogelio Sinán and I could really appreciate this phenomenon the night we read before an overflow crowd in one of Managua's public parks. Hundreds of people of all ages sat on the grass, intently following every word of the reading. Personally, I don't like reading my works aloud, nor do I enjoy hearing the works of others (perhaps because of my bad habit of solitary reading). That night I was afraid the program would drag on and that people would stay only out of politeness. Yet after the reading a group of young people came up to me to express their friendly annoyance that we had read so little. . . .

Finally, nearing the end of these fragments of memories, a few stray images stick in my mind. As everywhere in *our America,* the people's innocence, mingled with irony and humor, is an endless source of enchantment, like the sign of a humble store in the Oriental barrios: "Dimitri's Barbershop, Unisex Technique," which truly gives one pause.

Another store displays a sign to put up in an office: "Work

like the devil, don't talk like an angel." On a bit of open land in the center of town I saw a miserable shack of straw and sheet tin where an old woman sat in a hammock, patiently waiting for people to buy her homemade pastries. Above the shack a sign inexplicably read: "C.I.T." Nearby, in a vacant lot full of weeds and puddles, another sign announced: "Parking reserved for the clientele of C.I.T."

Because of so many things like this, as I leave Nicaragua more than anything else I feel tenderness, a tenderness which brings me back whenever I can possibly manage to come. I can't help but remember something Tomás Borge said, which sums up what I can't seem to express:

"You can't be a revolutionary without hands and eyes full of tenderness, without love for the poor and for the children."

Nicaragua from Within I

J U L Y   1 9 8 2

THE sea like a vast, mercurial glass. . . . I like to imagine that Darío might have written his poem looking out into the distance from the veranda of this bungalow where I am writing, in the vacation resort called El Velero (The Sailboat). Now that I think of it, the poet's city, León, is very near here. But none of this existed in Darío's day, except the vast, mercurial glass breaking on the coppery sand of the beach. The Sailboat, now a vacation resort for workers, came into being long after Darío's time and with a very different purpose than it has today. It was originally built as one of Somoza's clubhouses, where he came every now and then, I suppose, to meditate on how best to go on building clubhouses, utterly exclusive, in the most beautiful spots in the country, and more and more clubhouses—until the end we all know.

In this season they call winter, the Nicas are like the Cubans, assuming that only a foreigner or somebody with a terrific hangover would think of swimming in the ocean. They imagine the sea is cold, shot through with icebergs, yet this water is wonderfully warm, certainly warmer than anything I've ever experienced in the Mediterranean. And if you don't watch out in the broiling noonday sun, the lobsters will adopt you as one of their own. Anyway, since this is winter, it's very easy to get a bungalow by the sea. The Sailboat glides along with very few passengers on board. Yet even with so few guests, its pace is the same as at peak season. All services are in full swing: meals are served daily in the communal dining room (where you can also watch TV or play pool); occupied bungalows are cleaned daily; medical service is available three or four times a week. The resort is being expanded. Pipes are being laid. New bungalows are going up. It's so pleasant to cruise in this sailboat, where people smile frankly and spontaneously, and where *buenos dias* in the morning has a different ring than in the crowded cities. I especially enjoy seeing this former bastion of despotism transformed into a place where workers' families can rest and relax at very affordable rates.

A park called The Orchard-Garden stretches along the shore, extending between my bungalow and the sea, a "park" which exists more in the future than in the present. Though flowers and plants may be slow in springing up, the playthings for children have blossomed in all sorts of multicolored forms. Once again, ingenuity has made up for lack of materials: hammocks and slides have been put together out of planks, steel drums and bald tires, barely recognizable under brilliant coats of fresh paint. In the center is a sort of Mayan pyramid, with green and yellow steps—also former tires—which lead up to a platform. Once on top, instead of sacrificing to the gods, you can slide down a cement slide. But the kids tend to hop down frog-style, so as not to fry their little fannies on the griddle-hot cement. There's also a place to enjoy the view, with tables in the shade, and after dusk a white horse ambles over to sniff about the toys, as if with a vague nostalgia. And there are fireflies, and a tremendous peace.

But there's no peace on the Honduran border, from where news continues to arrive of attacks and counterrevolutionary skirmishes, which might be thought of as trial runs for the invasion that's been pending for so long. The Sandinistas are repelling these attacks but paying a brutal tribute in losses of all kinds. Simultaneously, the other governments of Central America are dancing to the tune of Washington, while brandishing the entire lexicon of "democracy" (as in usage in the north).

In two days, the Sandinistas will gather in Masaya to celebrate the third anniversary of liberation. Three hard years, inside and out, years of rebuilding with almost empty hands, years of respect for a political pluralism which from day one was exploited by those who mistrusted everything that meant a real advance in mass education, political consciousness and general enjoyment of the country's common wealth. It once occurred to me that while socialism claims to be international-ist, there is something which is even more internationalist: the bourgeoisie. The bourgeois are absolutely identical in every country in the world. A German bourgeois recognizes his French or Uruguayan counterpart more quickly than the socialists manage to recognize each other. That's why the bourgeoisie of Nicaragua is following exactly the same path and using exactly the same methods as did the bourgeoisie in Cuba.

When a tyranny becomes too harsh for them—that of a Batista or a Somoza—they help overthrow it, then join in the procession of victory. But stop right there, my friend! Heaven forbid that the great unwashed should take us at our word and want to meddle with our inheritance from *Papá,* or from *Grandpapá,* or with our profits from the multinationals, which you have to admit are bringing progress to the country, not to mention the very finest imports. . . .

I'll never forget something Fidel Castro said, following the triumphal entry into Havana, when the cars of the bourgeoisie were parading with revolutionary placards. He said to Che: "Within a month you'll see those placards come down." And they did. Here it has been no different.

But I was speaking of The Sailboat. It's time for lunch in the communal dining room. Beans, of course. You can bet on that. Beans and spicy ground meat, or fish, or eggs. And the ice-cold beer that is so incredibly refreshing in Nicaragua. The lunch plus coffee costs twenty-five córdobas (one dollar). The beer, three córdobas. *Buen appetito,* comrades!

Managua,
July 1982

Nicaragua from Within II

AUGUST 1982

I*N* Europe, with the news inevitably presented in bits and pieces, it tends to appear that the small countries of Latin America have nothing to do with each other. It is not always clear how events in these countries are entwined. Even in Central America, this interdependence has not always been evident. Today, however, it could not be more obvious. Each step forward in the Nicaraguan revolution, or step backward in the politics of Costa Rica, reverberates throughout the area. The whole region is opening outward. Its peoples are thinking in much broader terms, with vastly more political awareness. The armed struggle in Guatemala and El Salvador, the rising resistance in Honduras to the attempt at co-opting the army—these movements do not exist in isolation. Open any newspaper in Managua, and in the major front-page stories you will see the presence of all Central America. The mentality of the people is similar to that front page.

I say this after reading a recent interview by Claribel Alegría* and D. J. Flakoll* with Salvador Cayetano Carpio,* better known as Comandante Marcial, a figure already legendary in El Salvador, where after a lifetime of labor union struggles, persecution, imprisonment, torture and repeated exile, he and a group of comrades founded the People's Liberation Army-Farabundo Martí. Today, he's a member of the high command of the FMLN, the National Liberation Front (which also bears the name of Farabundo Martí). Right now, the FMLN is continuing to hold in check the government troops, which, despite massive aid from the United States, have come nowhere near stopping the advance of this guerrilla force, the armed representative of an entire people.

This interview contains several points which are essential to a better understanding of what Comandante Marcial calls regionalization. According to Marcial, this regionalization represents a shift in Washington's policy toward Central America and the Caribbean. U.S. interventions in the past (ranging from bankrolling friendly governments to armed invasions such as Sandino resisted in Nicaragua) were almost always localized, centered in particular places. But for some time now, Marcial observed, a global strategy has been replacing the isolated interventions and incursions. It's not by chance that a slow, insidious spider's web is being woven around *all* of Central America and the Caribbean. It's not by chance that the armies of the three "manageable" governments—Guatemala, Honduras, and El Salvador—are being supplied on a daily basis with every kind of antiguerrilla armament, not to mention technical assistance and vast quantities of cash. It's not by chance that the preposterously named Democratic Community of Central America has been thrown together, with (this will surprise no one) neither Cuba nor Nicaragua being asked to join. Nor is it chance that the new government of Costa Rica, once a model of good sense and good neighborliness, has stepped up its denunciations of the "Marxist advance," while in fact the issue is that of popular sovereignty.

Nor is it coincidental that under the guise of joint exercises, through which the North Americans have imparted plenty of Yankee know-how to their Honduran ally, the Hondurans are setting up a string of operational bases and military posts along the frontier with Nicaragua, exactly where the Somocista bands are sneaking across the border. These raids result in acts of sabotage, a general ravaging of the countryside, and random mass murder (such as the massacre at San Francisco del Norte).* Marcial has good reason to state the following: *We might say that we stand at the gates of war. It would be more accurate to say that all of Central America is now embroiled in war.*

The seriousness of the situation increases, as the mammoth spider of the north extends its web still further. But action leads to reaction, a dialectical effect which has apparently escaped the notice of Washington (as the rudimentary points of international law seem also to elude its notice). Today nobody in Central America considers himself isolated; the potent favor or equally potent enmity of the United States simply counts for too much.

Again, since the papers are a mirror of the peoples' understanding, the Nicaraguan daily papers are the best example of this regionalization of information. Every triumph or reversal of the popular forces in Guatemala or El Salvador, every favorable or unfavorable maneuver of Costa Rican or Honduran diplomacy, the recent events in Panama (one more link in the northern chain), the problems in Grenada or Belize—these things are all reported. Every event in Central America or the Caribbean is part of a global process and is seen as a positive or negative element in a game in which all the peoples of the region are engaged and for which they feel responsible.

Marcial thinks that the United States will finally be compelled to invade Central America militarily, an action he thinks will accomplish nothing. Why does he think this will happen? Because in whatever country the United States might land its forces, sooner or later it will find itself opposed, not only by the people of that country, but by the people of the entire region. Increasingly, that determination to fight back is shared by all who are fighting in this part of the world for independence and dignity—as Marcial, one of the most admirable examples of this struggle, knows so well.

Managua,
August 1982

Nicaragua from Within III
A U G U S T   1 9 8 2

TWO nights ago I was in one of the women's wards of the Dá-
vila Bolaños Hospital in Managua, visiting a fifteen-year-
old girl, a high school sophomore. I recognized her immediately, though the room was crowded with women patients,
because her picture has been in the papers here every day,
and hers is not a face to be forgotten or confused with anybody else's.

Everybody's talking about her smile, the same generous
smile which was on her lips as I approached her bed. People
speak of Brenda Rocha with a mixture of love and admiration,
but you can also sense their horror and, above all, their outrage at the reason why this child is in a hospital bed. Only a
few days ago Brenda lost her right arm. It was amputated five
inches from the shoulder.

In one of the most inaccessible regions of the country, near
the mineral deposits of Siuna, La Rosita and Bonanza, there's
a little town called Salto Grande. Like all the isolated communities of the interior, it is frequently threatened by bands of
Somoza's ex-Guard. Armed with weapons from abroad, these

roving bands have been murdering campesinos, robbing and destroying their villages and attacking the Sandinista militia which defend their towns. Brenda Rocha and a small group of *compañeros* from Bonanza were the militia responsible for the defense of Salto Grande. At age fifteen she had already taken part in the literacy campaign and joined the Sandinista Youth. She then became a member of the militia. As she herself says, with great naturalness, her task was to be ready for anything. On July 24 she was standing guard with her *compañeros* when a Somocista squad, superior in numbers and weaponry, stormed out of the hills and opened fire on the town.

In the ensuing battle, seven militia fighters died: six men and one woman. Bullets ripped through Brenda's right arm, but she went right on firing with her left. Finally, weak from loss of blood, she had to stop. By then the Somocistas were inside the town.

Lying face down on the ground, she pretended to be dead, and the attackers, fearing the arrival of Sandinista reinforcements, withdrew without touching her. Immediately the townspeople rushed to her aid, taking care of her until she could be moved to Managua, where it was necessary to amputate her arm. By the end of the month, the doctors say, she'll be able to go to the Soviet Union, where, by means of the most advanced surgical techniques, she'll be fitted with a prosthesis. For Brenda this means only one thing: being able to come home to her work, to carry on with her duties as a militiawoman.

As Brenda looked at me (with eyes that seemed so sweetly to refuse all pity, even all admiration), I reminded myself that the Nicaraguans, after so many years of all-out war, had known death so closely that their feelings for Brenda went deeper than their rejoicing that, by mere chance, she had escaped the fate which had brought down her comrades. For Brenda, as for all the Nicas—who think of her as a daughter, or a sister, or a future bride—the important thing is to accept what happened as part of the revolutionary effort, as one more proof of an invincible determination. That is why I believe that Brenda's smile, which everyone notices, is now engraved in memories and hearts with all the force of a call to arms, a revolutionary banner, or a militant song.

A friend who was with me that night in the hospital remarked that Brenda's smile was like the smile of a Giotto angel. True: but it's even more like the smile of the Angel of the Cathedral of Rheims, who looks down on us with an expression of mischievous grace, an expression almost of complicity. That angel seems to understand the whole world, which is why she is closer to us than those other angels who stand apart in an abstract purity. Brenda Rocha's face is the face of an angel. Yet nothing could be more beautifully human than this face which has looked death and horror in the eye and yet remains unmarked by rage or suffering. I suddenly understood why Brenda is such an inevitable symbol for the Nicas today: she is like Nicaragua. She *is* Nicaragua. Her fifteen years are the youth of the three years of the revolution. Her courage and serenity are the same I see day after day in these people, still standing together, steadfastly awaiting their enemies. Her shattered arm is the pound of flesh that has been paid and will go on being paid by the Nicaraguan people, so in love with light, with joy and with liberty. Yes, Brenda's smile is the smile of Nicaragua, which knows itself in her and makes her its own.

Managua,
August 1982

Nicaragua from Within IV
JULY 1982

I'M neither a foreign correspondent nor an expert in the geopo-
litics of Central America. These notes are meant to be read
between the lines of more detailed reports, rather like those
off-screen voices which enhance the meaning of an image, or
come to think of it, they may be more like those images which
somehow bring a rational argument to life. Lately, people
everywhere have been saying that the situation in Nicaragua
is grave, an inextricable part of a larger gravity which is con-
vulsing El Salvador, Guatemala and right now Honduras. But
what exactly is this grave situation?

For one thing, it's not immediately visible. Returning to
Managua I found myself in the midst of a rebuilding effort
whose enthusiastic pace was set by the Nicaraguan government right after the Sandinista victory. You can see the im-
provements in the quality of daily life, especially in nutrition
and sanitation. But many things are still lacking, things which
can be purchased only with credit and foreign exchange: vehi-
cles, spare parts, hospital supplies, medicines, the infrastruc-
ture needed for construction projects. These things are inevitably lacking, despite the donations of many countries East

and West. How could it be otherwise? The fact is that Nicaragua, when finally reclaimed by its rightful owners, was in pieces, like a shattered doll, or like a house ripped through by the most sinister of typhoons—not Flora, or Lucy, but *Somoza.*

The night I got in from Mexico I read in the papers that Sergio Ramírez had denounced a new U.S. plot to destabilize the Sandinista government and promote the eventual return to "democratic conditions" (Potomac-style). After putting on hold the grant of credits promised by Jimmy Carter after the Sandinista victory, the Reagan administration magnanimously decided to donate $5 million . . . to private enterprise in Nicaragua. When you realize that private enterprise is more or less synonymous with the conservative forces and/or U.S. interests, it's obvious this donation will hardly benefit the Nicaraguan people. What the Sandinista leadership would have devoted to projects for the general welfare, *to progress, not profit,* is once again thrust into the cesspool of personal, familial and corporate interests. *That* is why the situation is grave. Yet the danger is not really palpable. The invasion in the works for so long has not materialized. Everything seems to be going along at its usual clip. Nevertheless, the leaders of the government feel certain (they tell the people this with an admirable clarity, just as the people absorb this information with an admirable calm) that everyday the pincers are tightening and that the only way to forestall the worst is by throwing themselves wholeheartedly into something better—striving toward the highest possible level of political awareness, work and defense preparedness.

As happened in Cuba in one of its worst moments, natural catastrophe strikes on top of those disasters devised by enemies. The recent Nicaraguan floods have wrought damage which will be felt for at least two years in agriculture, transportation and housing. Needless to say, there's no money whatsoever to apply to these added problems. But it's reassuring to know that the current diplomatic efforts of various members of the government may help to strengthen the country's economic and political position. Comandante Daniel Ortega* in France and Spain, and Chancellor D'Escoto and Minister of Culture Ernesto Cardenal in other countries will create a clearer profile for Nicaragua, which is sometimes obscured on the complex chessboard of Central America.

We know too well how the international news services and the so-called liberal columnists (not to mention those of the real right wing) have been up to the same dirty tricks they played with Cuba. This same distortion is being echoed here by groups who feel their particular dogmas and economic interests are being threatened. With each passing day Nicaragua is more belligerently portrayed as a satellite of the USSR, with no acknowledgment whatsoever of the fact (I'm not even talking here about ideological choice) that the Soviet presence in the Caribbean was a direct result of that bumbling move by the United States which put Cuba in the position of either accepting an essential aid—Soviet oil—or in two weeks going under like a little paper boat. I repeat—it is possible, even probable, that the Soviet presence might eventually have been sought without such a dramatic motivation. And why not? But in those specific circumstances, and in the circumstances which confront Nicaragua today, to shout to the rafters about "Soviet interference" in the hemisphere is a hypocrisy comparable only to that of those self-styled democracies who refuse to recognize that the first half of that word contains what they fear the most, the true *demos,* which in Central America is gradually but truly entering history.

The situation in Nicaragua *is* grave. To understand that is a beginning. To try and lend a hand would be even better.

Managua,
July 1982

Greta Garbo's Feet

I'VE just finished reading a long article by a French journalist, Marcel Niedergang. This article, which appeared July 13 and 14 in the Paris *Le Monde,* contains impressions of his most recent trip to Nicaragua.

I've known Niedergang for a long time, and I want to make clear that I'm in no way questioning his sincerity or his good will toward the revolutionary process in Nicaragua. Unlike many self-styled correspondents who pronounce sweeping judgments after a whirlwind tour of a given country, Niedergang has been involved with Latin American issues for years. I respect him completely as a journalist and as a man—which is why I feel compelled to point out that he often writes in this article from a position that could give readers in Europe a false picture, an image that never breaks through to what is deepest and most vital in Nicaragua.

I'm not going to reproach somebody as busy as Niedergang for only now and then being able to spend a few days there. His vision must necessarily be fragmentary. But I can say this: if the partial view is to reveal the strongest colors of the whole, if the authentic spirit of the totality is to be captured, the writer must live with the people of a country; he must enter into the rhythms of many different lives; he must share their exertions, their sufferings and their joys, and he must do this under the most varied circumstances and over a period of days, weeks and even months.

I don't claim to know it all. I haven't spent enough time in Nicaragua myself to really understand the complex problems which crowd in upon the people daily, growing more urgent by the hour. My goal is simply to feel the heartbeat, to be as close as possible to the bare pulse of the emotions of the people. And right now that pulse is throbbing feverishly in response to the Somocista attacks and to the current U.S. efforts to destabilize the revolution.

Reading this article, with all this racing through my mind, what struck me most was its lack of any sense of a flesh-and-blood reality, of a visceral day-to-day existence. While Niedergang makes some interesting, even revealing, observations, his text falls yet again into the old European habit of reducing everything to a logical formula, to an almost geometrical analysis of positive and negative facts. It's like a chess game in which the skill or the clumsiness of each play is described, but in which the essential is never communicated: the passion of the players.

It strikes me as odd that somebody with Niedergang's experience of history should start his article with this title: "The Fervor Has Fallen Off in Estelí." He bases this conclusion almost entirely on the comments of a couple of shopkeepers. He then leaps to extend this conclusion from Estelí to Managua, then to the entire country. I'd like to come back to these sources and their arguments, but first I must point out the curious naiveté of this title. To begin with, Niedergang apparently confuses "fervor" with "enthusiasm," forgetting that in *all* revolutions, without exception, the victory, won at a terrible cost in suffering and bloodshed, gives rise to an enthusiasm, a euphoria, which is perfectly understandable. But the source of this emotion, the root cause of this delirious joy, is revolutionary fervor. Later, as days and months go by, the enthusiasm wanes, for obvious reasons: the return to mundane existence; the realization of just how many problems remain to be solved; the growing impact of the shortages and dangers which are part of every attempt to rebuild a country just emerging from the hellishness of war. So what remains is *fervor.* By which I mean faith—an unshakable faith in the cause of the revolution, an unshakable certainty that this cause will go forward, that the victory will be consolidated. This fervor goes beyond dancing and shouting in the streets. It goes beyond the euphoria and innocence of beginnings. It's more serious, and you can't see it clearly if you are not intimately connected to the heartbeat of the participants themselves.

If Niedergang reads this, he may think I am erring on the side of optimism. But five days ago when the news broke of the massacre of campesinos and militia fighters in San Francisco del Norte, savagely murdered by Somocistas coming out of Honduras, people poured into the streets in Managua. In fact, all over the country people were pouring into public squares to call for a *mano duro,* a "hard hand," and to reaffirm their will to defend the Sandinista revolution and the sovereignty of their country. If this spontaneity isn't fervor, I don't know what is. In the month I've been here I've already seen this phenomenon many times. I'll never forget the mass demonstration on July 19 in Masaya. What impressed me was not the gathering itself, which was part of the festivities for the third anniversary of the triumph, but the intelligent attention with which thousands and thousands of people listened to the long speech of Comandante Daniel Ortega. I could see by the quality of this attention that they understood the seriousness of the problems they were facing, and I could see their fervor, which certainly did not exclude enthusiasm, not at all. As workers and as Sandinistas, they were absolutely determined to defend and continue building what they'd won.

Now let's go back and look at the information which led Niedergang to conclude that "the fervor has fallen off in Estelí"—and everywhere else in the country. Interviewing a couple of petit bourgeois he discovers that "they are disappointed by the 'radical' direction of the Sandinista regime and worried by the mounting difficulties of daily life."

They are disappointed. Well, what would you expect from the bourgeoisie? This is exactly what happened in Cuba following the triumphal entry of *los barbudos*—the men with beards—into Havana. In the initial days the bourgeoisie applauds the elimination of a regime that was a bit too dangerous for their prosperity—the regime of a Batista or of a Somoza. But very quickly they grow frightened, realizing that the truly oppressed, the genuinely disinherited, have no intention of handing the reins of power over to them, or letting them call all the shots in a "liberal" or "democratic" government in which the quotation marks are more significant than the words. So the way to Miami is opened, after a period of hesitation in which the bourgeoisie is still hoping to come to power. When it finally realizes this is impossible, the all-too-familiar vocabulary is trotted out: "radicalization," "totalitarianism," and the inevitable "Marxist-Leninist." It happened in Cuba, it happened in Chile, it is happening now in Nicaragua. It has to happen, and it might as well happen and be done with.

The complaining couple also mention "the mounting difficulties of daily life." Here we enter another realm, that of decency and ethics. This seems to me a very serious point. Niedergang digs himself in even deeper with the following comments: "Life is getting harder and the future is full of anguish and uncertainty. Serious shortages exist: basic medications are not available; sugar is being rationed; the gas stations are closed on Sundays." Reading this, a European reader would naturally assume that these problems are occurring *because* of the policies of the Sandinista leadership. He will then imagine he understands why "the fervor is falling off in Estelí." But the fact is that many people outside Nicaragua do not know the actual conditions which Nicaragua was left in by Somoza. Or how almost immediately after July 19, as also happened in Cuba in 1959, the United States initiated its policy of economic blockade, including the freezing of credits. One more attempt to starve to death any "trespassers" in its famous backyard.

But did Niedergang go to visit the hospitals right after the Sandinista victory? Did he see men, women and children lying on the floor, since no beds were available? Did he observe that not even aspirin was obtainable? Everything which international solidarity has donated toward medical relief has been immediately turned over to the hospitals and pharmacies, and the situation has greatly improved. But in so little time, with virtually no foreign exchange, how could basic medications be anything other than lacking? And let's not kid ourselves—this hypercritical couple know exactly what the situation is. That's why I'm talking about decency and ethics. No matter what their class or economic interests, the enemies of the Sandinistas are acting in a completely dishonest, unethical manner, blaming the government for shortages and inadequacies, the real causes of which they know perfectly well.

Niedergang notes with satisfaction that the literacy campaign has been a success. He cites statistics and dates that should be very informative to European readers. Nevertheless, he remarks in closing that according to several international experts the incredible effort made by the people to educate themselves is falling apart. Why? For "lack of continuity" in being carried out. "Because the government is vacillating between primary education and adult literacy work, unsure which should be given priority." When I see the Minister of Education, I'll ask him about this last point, but as for "lack of continuity," can these experts possibly be unaware of the actual conditions in Nicaragua, where from one day to the next an invasion from Honduras is expected? At this very moment the United States is carrying out military exercises with the Honduran army, while bands of Somocistas and other mercenaries continually cross the border to rape, murder and pillage. If Nicaragua's enemies can point to any success, it is this: they have forced the country to divert resources into defense, away from work, production and education. It's easy to talk about literacy in Europe, where every few blocks there's a school with more pencils and blackboards than could ever be used. Here in Nicaragua a pencil is a small treasure, and it grips my heart when I remember seeing in Comandante Borge's house a cardboard box full of pencils, which he was going to take by helicopter to distribute among the Miskito

Indians on the Atlantic Coast. This detail says it all. How many "objective facts" fall flat compared to the force of these small things, which move us and propel us forward.

Finally, what strikes me most about Niedergang's article is the feeling of negativity which I think defines it from the title on. Undoubtedly he's right in many instances, and plenty of Sandinistas would agree with him. But he fails to give proper weight to the positive side of the process, the tremendous achievements in three years, the steady gains being made in so many different fields, despite all the shortages and problems. To learn about these positive gains, about all sorts of ongoing or successfully completed projects, he need only have read the newspapers systematically, including the opposition paper, *La Prensa.* He would have learned about new hospitals, new markets, new social services, new methods of moving food about the country. Not to mention the work of the extraordinary publishing house Nueva Nicaragua, which is getting books into even the most remote parts of the country. And the new magazines, and cultural programs of every sort. There is also music, and the encouragement of tourism for working families. I'm writing this, in fact, at the vacation center for workers called The Sailboat. And so many other things . . . Why not at least mention a few of the most important of these in order to balance a report which, for want of this positive side, tends to melancholy and pessimism? It's like somebody describing a person by mentioning the glasses, the blemishes, a missing tooth . . . but failing to point out that the person in question is twenty-five years old, in vibrant health and in possession of a perfectly proportioned body. When I was young it was said that Greta Garbo had huge feet. I thought, maybe so, but the rest of her is like a goddess.

Niedergang also raises the issue of the assistance Nicaragua has received from foreigners, mainly Cubans, on various major projects. This sort of internationalism almost always clashes with a certain idea of nationalism. This sort of tension is not new to French readers who aren't particularly happy with the presence of Africans and Arabs in their country (although very different causes have led to these foreign presences). It may be true that some Nicaraguans have had similar reservations—for political, religious or simply chauvinistic reasons. On the other hand, most Nicaraguans will never forget the work of those *compañeros* in hospitals and in literacy brigades. Niedergang alludes to "serious incidents," in particular in Bluefields on the Atlantic coast. I would like to recall that in highly refined Paris we need look no further than the nearest suburb to learn of incidents even more "serious" involving Frenchmen and Algerians. Nobody has the right to take a situation specific to the Atlantic coast and represent it as typical of the entire country.

We can be sure that the United States and the counterrevolutionaries will not let pass any opportunity to vilify Cuba's assistance, which they immediately described as pure and simple ideological infiltration, denying any genuine wish to be of help, or any real feeling of brotherhood. Their goal was to create the image of a second Cuba, having distorted for more than twenty years the image of the first. This, it must be stated, was accomplished with the help of the Cubans themselves, who have not always had the will or the expertise to take on that gigantic campaign of distortion which has cost them so much ground, for example, in France.

As the article proceeds to address problem after problem after problem, the lack of balance finally becomes intolerable.

Although Niedergang has positive things to say about agrarian reform (which he rightly judges to be essential if the people on the land are ever to own that land and its produce), he devotes the lion's share of his commentary to the opinions of Sandinista opponents, limiting statements by Sandinista leaders to a few meager lines, which are not always sufficiently to the point. For example, one of the colleagues of Alfonso Robelo* (exmember of the government and now an opponent of the Sandinistas) is given space to put forward various political and economic criticisms, while the reader is given no information whatever on the Sandinista side of the question. To repeat, I don't think Niedergang is writing in bad faith. But he certainly does tend to provide us with uneven doses of his various sources of information, so uneven that finally it seems he himself has fallen into the trap and is viewing Nicaragua from the trench of the opposition.

At first glance, this may seem like a petty thing (though nothing is petty in this game which is life or death for Nicaragua) but why describe Comandante Bayardo Arce* as someone "with a cigar and a beard *à la* Fidel Castro"? Nowhere does he refer to Mr. Robelo's colleague as "smoking cigarettes and clean-shaven *à la* Ronald Reagan." Why these psychological insinuations, which are the stock in trade of the United States, the supreme master at creating stereotypes in the minds of its citizens?

Speaking of Reagan, Niedergang's article ends on a very positive and I might say encouraging note, since he makes definite reference to the policy of the U.S. government, describing it as aggressive and equivocal. He also states that the measures taken by the Nicaraguan government are the only appropriate response under the circumstances. Niedergang might have stated this in even stronger terms had he written his article ten days later, after the attempt to blow up the oil refinery at the Port of Corinto and in light of the massacre at San Francisco del Norte, and of the joint maneuver of the U.S. and Honduran armies, and of the flagrant violation of the Torrijos-Carter accords on the Panama Canal.

Now I, too, must close these remarks, which I've tried to make as constructive as possible. Who can say how I would end if I were writing another week or two in the future? Here in Nicaragua, we are living from one minute to the next, and the future waits on another roll of the dice of history. But we *can* speak of what is past, and we have the obligation to do so without in any way distorting the facts.

Managua,
July 1982

Ten Points

1.

A NEWSPAPER with the prestige of *Le Monde* of Paris has no right to be irresponsible. But it has been just that. And on a major issue. The historical crisis of Nicaragua has been treated with utmost frivolity in an article of last year by Marcel Niedergang and in a more recent article by Charles Vanhecke. How can such flagrant bias be permitted? It is well known that these signatures carry weight; anything these men write is believed to the letter by most readers of *Le Monde*.

Last year I sent a reply, a sort of corrective to the slant of this first article, but my remarks were never published. Perhaps these comments, which I'm writing from Nicaragua, will come to the attention of readers of *Le Monde*. (Incidentally, I spend a good deal more time here than the writers in question, who rush to pass judgment after only the briefest visit.)

Anyway, I refer here only to Mr. Vanhecke's article, and I'll do so as briefly as possible.

2.

FIRST, the title of the article: "The Confiscated Revolution." This is a prime example of what we might call European "purism," a phenomenon more than amply demonstrated by the case of the Cuban Revolution. Phase one of this purist reaction: Hurrah for the Revolution! Hooray for the Revolution! Viewed from a flawed and nostalgic Europe, the events in Cuba seem bathed in pristine light. It's the noble savage all over again—purity, an ideal liberty—but the purity of a revolution lasts only fifteen days, as Jean Cocteau once said (a writer, by the way, who is not as frivolous as some people think). The revolution then enters a phase of internal divisions. It discovers its limits and all its dregs and dross. It rips into itself and defends itself with all it has in it of the human, all too human. The reaction of European purists (phase two): What a disappointment! (Disappointment automatically generates hostility, open or veiled.) Third phase (the present): The purists, disillusioned, vent their spleen by denouncing and deploring mistakes and failures. *And they see only the mistakes and failures,* or almost only. Niedergang and Vanhecke have played out exactly this pattern in the case of Nicaragua.

3.

ERGO, the revolution has been *confiscated.* By whom? By the Sandinistas, evidently. The Archbishop of Managua* and the director of *La Prensa* seem to think so, anyway. They tell Vanhecke how the church and the bourgeoisie also fought for the revolution and that now they are being shunted aside. What they fail to mention is that the church and the bourgeoisie entered the battle only in the final stages of a twenty-year struggle against Somoza and his National Guard, a battle the Sandinistas fought from the very beginning, under almost unbelievably harsh conditions. Failure to acknowledge this critical difference and to claim today a total parity with respect to the Sandinistas has only one name: cynicism.

4.

VANHECKE is apparently not pleased by the sympathy the Sandinistas express for Cuba. But he is silent regarding the fact that after the victory, when the country was receiving from nowhere else the support it needed to emerge from ruins, Cuba sent its best literacy teachers and doctors to Nicaragua.

How not and why not love a fraternal country which acts in this way? Ah (this in a very low voice), but behind it all looms the Russian bear. . . . Exactly. And who is prodding the Russian bear if not the United States, as it did in Cuba when the economic blockade would have strangled that island within three months? Paradoxically, Washington has been the best catapult for the USSR to project its influence—which it has every right to do, ideologically speaking—into the Caribbean and Central America.

Nor does Vanhecke bother to inform us of the other sources of aid to Nicaragua. To mention only a recent case: we might assume he doesn't know that following a visit by a Danish commission, which studied Nicaragua's problems in depth, Denmark donated no less than $1 million to aid in the task of reconstruction. Evidently the Danes have their own idea of this "confiscated revolution." Or are they all mad, like Hamlet?

5.

THIS biased presentation of information is unforgivable. Of course there are—and should be— criticisms! But there is no excuse for citing *at length* the criticisms of members of the opposition (who belong to a certain church, not to mention a certain class which is terrified of losing its privileges) while at the same time ignoring all the admirable Sandinista achievements in social welfare, sanitation and education. Does the reader of *Le Monde* realize that Nicaragua does not have a single fine arts museum and that a month ago a splendid collection of over three hundred works was inaugurated in Managua, works donated by artists of international stature? Did Vanhecke visit the shopping centers, models of community worthy of any developed country? Did he visit the settlements of the Miskito Indians, whom the revolution has managed to wrench away from their ancestral hostility or indifference (legitimate) to those they still call "the Spaniards"? Their controversial resettlement was necessary to prevent the Somocistas on the border from misleading them, forcibly recruiting them, or slaughtering them, as is still happening now on a weekly basis. Was Vanhecke interested in agrarian reform? (Niedergang was, and it's right to point that out.) Did he visit the poetry workshops or the publishing house, which is bringing out paperbacks at dirt-cheap prices? Did the Archbishop show him any of that?

6.

CERTAINLY many things can be criticized; we are not blind idealists. One of the most thorough critics is Comandante Tomás Borge. Or Sergio Ramírez. Or Ernesto Cardenal. Or Chancellor Miguel D'Escoto. But Vanhecke hears only the criticism of the director of *La Prensa,* who tells him this: "The leaders of the revolution are guerrilla fighters who still have the dirt from the mountains on their boots." He says this of men such as those I've just named, who are every bit as intellectual or more intellectual than he is. Or he listens to Mr. Calero,* entrepreneur and one of the leaders of the Conservative party, who had the gall to say: "The Sandinistas are inept leaders who are running the economy into the ground. Whose economy? That of the Caleros, the businessmen, of course. But another economy is being born here in Nicaragua.

7.

MRS. BALTODANO, director of a human rights association, told Vanhecke that twenty people have disappeared in Nicaragua since the Sandinista victory, implying that the authorities were responsible. Is Vanhecke unaware of what I have come to know in my five or six trips to this country—that the counterrevolutionaries are killing hundreds of people? An entire defenseless village is massacred by enemies of the regime: no mention. A taxi driver arrested by the police turns up dead and with signs of torture: seventeen indignant lines. Is it possible that the reporting of violent acts can be this unbalanced?

8.

LA PRENSA deplores the state of emergency, but Vanhecke explains none of the reasons which make it necessary at this time. Perhaps he thinks the revolution can defend itself by giving a completely free rein to CIA infiltrators. Or to those who resent the agrarian reform for expropriating their vast estates? Or to an Archbishop who mistrusts the revolution, fearing the influence of activist priests who have taken the side of the people?

9.

CENSORSHIP: Crocodile tears, outcries and indignation. In Managua I read *La Prensa* every day. Whenever possible the liberation movement of El Salvador, so inextricably connected to the destiny of Nicaragua, is described as "Marxist," exactly as in the papers in the United States. When a husband caught a priest in bed with his wife, *La Prensa* described this priest as a victim of a plot to discredit the bishopric, while the Sandinista papers published the confession of the woman in question, made before a judge, admitting the priest was simply her lover and had been for some time. On at least two occasions I was able to verify that notices of the attacks and murders on the frontiers were published as secondary news items by *La Prensa;* in one case the front page was given over to a photo of a society party, or it may have been an athletic event. Is that any way to defend a country threatened by the most serious dangers?

10.

AND so on, *ad nauseam*. Perhaps these brief remarks may be useful to the readers of *Le Monde* and to the newspaper itself.

Managua,
January 1983

Dignity and Beauty

*K*NOW *thyself.* . . . Easy to say. Still easier to believe it is possible. Then, later, in moments of rupture, of implosion, of a fall into oneself, one discovers something else: infinite skins of the onion. We'll never come to the end of tearing off the veils, from the seven veils of Salome to the prodigious cave-delving of psychoanalysis. Deeper, always deeper, the center refuses to let itself be seen. We are far from many things, but from nothing are we further than from ourselves.

High-flown thoughts, as you see, perhaps because spun out at an altitude of eight thousand meters aboard a plane which is taking me back to my beloved Managua. All these months I've wanted daily to be back, to add my strength once again to the Sandinista effort, to learn more about this liberating process, then later to disseminate that knowledge as my way of doing what I can to counteract the many lies and half-truths circulating in Europe. I confess I've been afraid of remaining away, for fear the worst might happen when I was out of the country, and that I might not be able to get back in—everybody knows that the Honduran frontier is a colossal sword of Damocles. . . .

Touching ground now in Managua, something also touches ground in another part of myself, and I feel that what I most want to see is the museum of painting and sculpture inaugurated in December with the works donated by hundreds of excellent Latin American artists. After a quick look around, I would plunge into the streets, as so many times before, making the rounds of friends who would brief me on the current situation and send me off to the most critical spots of the moment. But first the museum. I really can't say why. (Know thyself. What a joke!)

Like a brutal and necessary corrective, I was hardly out of the airport with Comandante Tomás Borge when reality hit me in the face: we had not gone half a kilometer when we saw a funeral procession coming toward us and heard the Sandinista chants of the small group of mourners accompanying the body of a combatant fallen three days earlier on the Honduran border, one of many who have died and are still dying under the bullets of the exguardsmen.

Only much later did I remember the museum. There, I told myself, life goes on. There, in those works of art, is another kind of incentive to go forward, to surpass oneself in every realm. Carmen Waugh, the Chilean *compañera* who had organized the museum, took me to the Rubén Darío Theater, where the greater part of the works are temporarily exhibited, awaiting a permanent location, not so easily come by in a city still showing countless scars of the earthquake, and without resources to install a modern museum.

But that's how it is in Nicaragua, where things get done any which way and later are improved. I can't think of any other example of such an enormous and valuable collection of art works preexisting a museum to house them. But for now the public strolls through the halls, resigned to the dim lighting, exclaiming to friends or beginning a first silent dialogue with an art which is aggressively contemporary and which provokes everything an advanced art should provoke: attraction, revulsion, antagonism—the taking of whatever stance is necessary to raise the imagination to its highest power. Then, a bit hoarse from talking, the visitors leave the exhibition with something new and distinct in their memories, something which will remain, unconsciously modifying their inner vision, refining their taste and encouraging them to reject every cheap thing which passes for art and beauty, a cheapening which won't disappear overnight.

Nicaragua has magnificent artists, both "educated" and "primitive." This museum should stimulate interest in their works, wherever they are on display, even in the artists' studios. Each new discovery teaches the eye—the aesthetic vision. And the international *always* enhances the experience of the national.

Let me mention something else which seems to me quite important. Though the collection already exists, open to the public without charge, almost everything remains to be done—and I'm confident the Nicas will do it as soon as possible, despite the spectacular difficulties they face. But a descriptive catalogue is especially needed, so a public unversed in contemporary art can start to get a sense of the various aesthetic currents, and of the personalities of artists as famous as Lam, Matta, Le Parc, Soto . . . the list goes on. Another thought: artists and teachers might bring their students and guide them through this tangle of forms, colors, rhythms. The literary supplements might promote a desire to tour the museum. Actually, the term *museum* has never appealed to me, with its faint odor of Egyptian mummies or ivory towers. Why not call it the House of Latin American Art, or something equally welcoming and neighborly? Young Nicaraguan painters, engravers and sculptors might act as volunteer tour guides, talking with visitors, taking them around, helping them as *compañeros* to get their bearings in this new territory.

I was thinking, leaving the museum, how this is the *first* in the country, and how already Latin American solidarity has made it one of the richest and most representative on the continent. The fact that genuine beauty of such scope should be exhibited in Nicaragua today is for me the best symbol of this country's present and future. There's no rational explanation for how this museum is giving people strength, intensifying their determination as they fight for a free and dignified life. There can be no revolution without beauty and poetry: two sides of an essential medallion.

Managua,
January 1983

Vigil in Bismuna

I*N* the marshy lowlands of the northeast, a short distance from the Honduran border, where an undeclared war is raging on, there's a tiny speck on the map: Bismuna, ruin of a Miskito Indian town and the site only ten days ago of a ferocious battle between Sandinista border guards and a band of counterrevolutionaries.

At almost exactly the same time, a group of some twenty U.S. citizens of different origins, faiths and professions were landing in Managua with the declared intention of holding a "vigil for peace" as near as possible to the war zone. They had come to protest the "Big Pine" maneuvers being carried out by U.S. troops in a joint exercise with the Hondurans.

The Salvadoran poet Claribel Alegría, her husband and I decided to accompany this group and share their vigil. The first phase of our trip (endorsed, of course, and facilitated by the Sandinista government) brought us as far as Puerto Cabezas on the isolated and hard-to-reach Atlantic coast. When we arrived, the first thing Comandante William Ramírez said to us was this: "You people are completely crazy!

Up until yesterday there's been a hell of a fight going on in Bismuna, and that is exactly where it occurs to you to go. I don't know if I can authorize your trip—I'll let you know tomorrow—but if the answer is yes, you can bet I'll be going with you, because I'm crazy too, when this kind of thing's going on."

Following this declaration, which we all agreed was thoroughly sensible, we had to wait. This gave us a chance to look around Puerto Cabezas, the second most important city of that distant and strategic Atlantic region. For the first time in those perilous days the North Americans were able to see the spirit of the local people. That very night huge, crackling bonfires were lit on the street corners, while crowds gathered to sing Sandinista or traditional songs, to hear poems by local writers, and to show their support for the ongoing defense alert, more urgent than ever on this coast, so vulnerable to enemy infiltration.

The next morning we finally started out for Bismuna, where Sandinista border guards awaited us to provide security and to brief us on what to do in case of attack. We were put up in the abandoned shacks of the Miskito Indians—now living in one of the new settlements, intended to protect them from further attack. Our encampment, where the principal enemies were insects and a sun like molten lead, became the site of that vigil for peace, so near to the suspect maneuvers.

The visitors made contact easily with the Sandinista soldiers, thanks to the excellent interpreters who accompanied our group, and all of us got a good look at the situation on the border. Going out to the site of the recent battles, we saw smoke still sifting from burnt out shacks and pastureland;

some gruesome traces of the fighting were still visible among the ruins.

All sorts of colorful anecdotes filled our vigil days, and the nights were enlivened by gatherings where the young soldiers heard Norma Elena Gadea, tireless singer of the Nicaraguan song, and got to know their surprising visitors better, talking and sharing food and mosquitoes with equal fraternity.

The second night a sort of alert was in force, which made it necessary to sleep with our boots on, ready to run to a trench into which we were under orders to hurl ourselves in case of bombardment. But we soon saw that the defeat suffered by the counterrevolutionaries in recent days was sufficient for the moment to keep them at a distance.

WE later learned that news of the vigil had been reaching the United States, where many people must have been deeply moved by the dramatic symbolism of our action. Meanwhile, massive deployments of troops, ships, planes and even U.S. submarines were maneuvering in the region with the Honduran army. On this side a small group of twenty women and men were mounting a silent, peaceful vigil, holding aloft signs against nuclear war and in protest of their country's intervention in Central America. Once again the small David stands up to the monumental Goliath.

Never have the stars of the sultry, tropical night seemed to me more brilliant or more beautiful than as I kept watch with my North American *compañeros;* never have I felt more certain that the future of Central America would belong to its struggling peoples, from Guatemala to El Salvador. I said to one of those momentary yet permanent friends: "Some day we'll be able to look at the sky just to contemplate these stars—there will be no enemy planes."

The smoke from our cigarettes was sweeter and more fragrant in the inclusive silence around our midnight fire.

Nicaragua,
February 1983

Return to Solentiname

S*EVEN* years isn't a long time, but in the history of new Nicaragua they are like seven-league boots which, with enormous
strides, are carrying this Pulgarcito* of Central America into
the future. Perhaps that's why, when I accepted a friend's
invitation to return to the region of the great lake, I thought of
my first trip in 1976. There's something very distant about
the memory of those days, as if somehow *everything* began on
that date when I first set foot on the archipelago of Solentiname and entered, in secret and in the middle of the night,
the community of Ernesto Cardenal.

Prodigious acceleration of history! Culminating on July 19,
1979, and opening today on the vast panorama of a truly
popular process, which has already achieved so many tangible
successes—tasks completed or being completed in the midst
of what is still poverty and still the tropics, these persistently
topical tropics, with all their drawbacks and holdovers from
the past, that exacerbated machismo— This is Latin America
in its most torrid zone, Nicaragua as violently sweet as the
sudden sunsets when pink and orange bleed into velvet green

and night descends, fragrant and dense, thick with tiger eyes.

Speaking of tigers, there's another tiger here, but—before getting to that—let me talk about my trip to San Carlos and the launch which took me down the San Juan River to Santa Fe, to that house of friends where for endless hours I would watch the broad waters, teeming with fish and festooned with islands of floating plants, waters idly seeking their outlet in the Atlantic.

Looking out at the river I thought of Langston Hughes' poem *(I've seen rivers . . .)* and of how time and space seemed strangely to fuse along that flowing road (as the ancient Egyptians called the Nile). I regret that I'm not better at describing landscapes. I would have liked to send the reader off into that languid heat, scored by the fine white of herons on the shores of the San Juan. I'd like the reader to feel what Europe so long ago lost: the vague fear of the unknown, of the mystery that begins on river shores and which the double green curtain of jungle and mangrove swamp hides from the eye. No point in consulting the map, where uncertain references show tributaries, hills and volcanoes, with rarely any hint of human life—a scattering of tiny towns in a sonorous solitude, whose sounds are calls of alarm: the agorero bird, the sudden roar of wild animals, the jeering screech of monkeys. Awesome shades of Orellana, Gonzalo Pizarro, Lope de Aguirre, their almost unthinkable courage as they penetrated for the first time this watery world which still today teems with danger and death: no longer the poisoned arrow whistling out of the brush, but the grenade of the counterrevolutionary, the military ambush which has cost so many lives in Nicaragua.

Later we went on horseback to Solentiname. I mean, we

crossed the vast lake in a launch that galloped on breakneck waves which forced us instinctively to seek out footholds or restraints of some kind so as not to be wildly thrown about. Then the archipelago, and the island which sheltered Ernesto Cardenal's community. Signs of the Somocista vandalism were still visible: the burnt out craft workshop, the ransacked houses—yet everything is being rebuilt, white and sweet as in those brightly detailed paintings the world now knows. The church was left untouched, and the delectable childlike decorations on the walls still shine with all the colors of the local fish, hens, thatched huts, alligators and little airplanes. Cardenal will return in April to a house they are finishing for him now. The guest house is already in use. Over a long lunch with friends we saw the lake rise under a wind that put our return in danger.

But who wanted to return?

I walked alone for a while through the meadows, where in 1976 I felt for the first time the call of Nicaragua, the beginning of a communion, of a pact then dark and secret.

Reluctantly I boarded the launch which would take us back to San Carlos. I was still in a reverie of memories and sensations, cast about by time, the river and the lake, when a tremendous jolt hurled us all into a reality which showed no promise of being agreeable.

The launch shuddered to a sudden halt. There was rushing about, the inevitable cries, then came the almost absurd explanation: an enormous shad had been trapped in the propeller and sliced into a bloody mess of flesh and scales which had to be laboriously picked out of the blades. The size of that kamikaze shad! But finally we reached San Carlos, where a small plane was waiting to fly us back to Managua. I thought of the shad and the tiger. I looked back at the broad coppery-brown current of the San Juan. Here, disproportion has been the measure of all things, as everywhere in Nicaragua.

Fastening the seatbelt (which seems to me so pointless in light aircraft), I thought of how tiny Nicaragua is, this land of people living with tigers, with shad that can stall a big launch, this land of people who test themselves every day against a much larger power. Looking back from the air, I could see Solentiname beneath a sky of amber dusk. There lies peace. The beauty of the wise and innocent popular art will flourish again, with shad and tigers painted or carved by children, women and fishermen. Everything is searching out its way here, its difficult equilibrium. This tropical land will not always be topical, making headlines, burdened with poverty and with war. Someday this land will be the tropics for a people who are truly free, inside and out.

Not for a long time yet, *compañero.* But Pulgarcito has pulled on his walking boots once and for all.

Nicaragua,
February 1983

The Writer and His
Task in Latin America

TEXT OF A SPEECH

I *APOLOGIZE* if these remarks sound too much like a lecture. Looking out from this podium, seeing so many dear and admired faces, I feel like I'm joining a group of friends to have a conversation. But I know myself well enough to realize that the mere fact of standing at a podium, which puts me physically above everyone else (also the case at ground level), is enough to deprive me of all verbal spontaneity, and sometimes even of coherence. Incapable of improvising a single line of a speech, I've had to write out what I would much rather have expressed with that ease and fluency I admire in others.

Most of us here have been grappling for years with the issue which brings us together today: the task of the writer in Latin America. It's hardly necessary to reiterate ideas now clear to every responsible intellectual. By responsible I mean those who are aware of the struggle for freedom and self-determination and who have decided to be part of that struggle, or to help consolidate the victory if this battle has already been won.

Fortunately, the old polemics on the "writer's commitment" have given way to a concrete problem: What should we be doing that we aren't already doing? How, as intellectual workers, can we be more politically effective? How can we invent and apply new forms of contact which, however slowly, can begin closing the enormous gap now separating writers from those as yet unable to be their readers?

Though most of us lack talent in the practical arena (we needn't be ashamed, since our work is in another realm), nobody can have failed to note the importance of the more pragmatic phase now beginning. Theoretical analyses have now been exhausted, and the way is clear for action, for direct involvement. As literary engineers, as planners and architects of words, we've had more than enough time to imagine and calculate the arc of the bridges so urgently needed to bring the intellectual product to its potential consumer. The time has now come to construct these bridges in reality, to strike out into the open to forge a tangible communication, a literary vitality for ourselves and a vital literature for our people.

As symbol and reality, the bridge is almost as old as man. A poem, or a piece of music, or a novel, or a painting, has always been a bridge. What is new is the idea that those novels, paintings and pieces of music might extend to another shore, where nothing like them has ever been experienced.

Though editors provide bridges between writers and readers, beyond the perimeters of that traffic stretch wastelands of isolation and lack of communication, perhaps on a smaller scale in a country like Spain, but in frightening proportions throughout Latin America. Hence our task as intellectuals is to confront this problem head on, a problem either ignored or made light of by intellectuals ensconced in a complacent urban environment, a world of elite humanistic notions. Governments and politicians are no better, entrenched in their capitals, shuttling back and forth between metropolitan centers, light-years removed from the vast multitudes who surround them in silence: a silence of ignorance, oppression, isolation and otherness.

Three weeks ago I was in Nicaragua once again, to be with those who understand better than anyone the disastrous effects of a certain notion of culture, a notion based on the time-honored principle that the ignorance of the many increases the wealth of the few.

For three years a top priority of the Sandinista government has been the elimination of illiteracy. Mass literacy is the first step toward incorporating all the people into the vast body of human thought represented by the written word. It's no accident that writers of the stature of Ernesto Cardenal and Sergio Ramírez are members of this government; or lovers of poetry and the visual arts such as Miguel D'Escoto and Tomás Borge; or that one of its young guerrilla comandantes, Omar Cabezas, has published a first-person account of his experience in the struggle against Somoza, a narrative written with a rare literary skill; or that a virtual galaxy of writers and artists are working together to solve the tough daily problems of the country. It's no accident that the Nicas are among the first to build intellectual bridges between cities and hinterland, between writers (who until now had only a few predictable readers) and the masses of people who from one day to the next are beginning to understand that life is more than just surviving, that work need not end every night in an exhausted sleep, that the process of thinking can go beyond received ideas, atavistic notions and prejudices.

I allude here to Nicaragua in some detail, since my recent

experience there has made clear just how urgent and crucial our work as writers can be. To begin with, Nicaraguan intellectuals seem to be more effectively integrating their intellectual work with their multiple roles as leaders, administrators and participants in the endless meetings, panel discussions and mass demonstrations. If this seems feasible only in a context of revolutionary reconstruction, it nevertheless highlights by contrast how thoroughly writers in other countries are hog-tied by conventions which set them apart from everybody else. Wherever we may live, the Nicaraguan example makes us ask if we should not be projecting our works much more forcefully upon the Latin American scene, whenever possible with a physical presence. We might alter the nature of our works, so they might be read more widely, perhaps entering more readily into circles where they could be of use, yet we must do this without in any way violating the true character of our expression. I need hardly stress that I'm not advocating facility or that simplification which some call for in the name of "reaching the people," not realizing that all intellectual paternalism is a disguised form of contempt.

Intellectual vanguards cannot be restrained. Nobody will ever get a true writer to lower the standard of his creation; the serious writer knows that man's emblem in history and in culture is an ascending spiral. But our task is to encourage and facilitate access to culture—immediate or mediated. Only then can this spiral be the creation of everyone; only then can it ascend in an exponential acceleration, only then can each— creator and receiver—have the power to give of his or her highest potential.

But theories, as I have said, are behind us. The moment is at hand for action. Let me speak as concretely as possible.

Not long ago, in a speech still kicking up dust in certain arenas, the French Minister of Culture—in Mexico—stated that a culture disassociated from the deepest impulses of its peoples, in all their ethnic and political diversity, is not truly a culture at all. Not a new idea, but for the first time it has the force of being proclaimed by a government ready to put it into practice, hurling forward this idea like a challenge to all the sham cultures which Latin America has suffered to excess— cultures of stagnation, if not outright destabilization of values. This critical attitude, limited before to an enclave of intellectuals (and expressed in books, lectures or graduate seminars), is now ringing out like a trumpet call through all Latin America: an entire continent of cultures which have been subjugated, shunted aside or assimilated, a continent as well of absurdly elitist cultures, cultures which exist only for the educated few. Therefore, when asked to speak of our task, I can only say that we must transcend the outworn idea of culture as an immobile property; we must attempt the impossible and try to *mobilize* culture, to make of it an element of collective life, of give and take, of change and exchange, such as happens with consumer goods, with bread, bicycles, shoes.

But how, I ask myself, how can we, as intellectuals, extract the living germ from that husk which in the elitist mind is inseparable from culture itself, from all poetry, from all art?

DEVISING NEW FORMS

SOME glimmerings of an answer to these questions have recently appeared. Most responsible writers in Latin America participate in one way or another (apart from their books) in political life, some directly, as in the case of the Nicaraguans already mentioned, some in a parallel way, through journalistic work. (García Márquez is an excellent example.) Other writers work with human rights or solidarity organizations, taking part in various tasks of support or denunciation as the case requires. It seems to me an excellent initial step for writers to work with lawyers, political leaders, economists and sociologists. The Bertrand Russell Tribunal is a good example of this type of action.

Nevertheless, this growing involvement of intellectuals with the very stuff of history, with the mass movements of Latin America, has up to now been limited, partly by the specialized nature of these activities and partly by the obstacles put in the way of reaching out to the masses, roadblocks set up by the oppressive regimes of our continent and by its ever-watchful godfather in the north. Hence it is urgent that we devise new forms of contact. A whole new spectrum of communications needs to be created at every level. The time has now come for a thorough self-criticism of our stereotyped attitudes toward our own profession. Or vocation, if you prefer. (And here I must add that writing is not only a vocation, but a means of transport and communication.)

GOING BEYOND WORDS

THIS might seem puerile, but if, as the saying goes, the child is father of the man, why hold back in the name of an adult caution which often doesn't get us anywhere anyway? So far I've abstained from literary allusions or digressions, and I trust one exception will underscore this restraint. But I would like to mention that in 1812 the poet Shelley felt exactly what we are feeling today. His desire to spread his revolutionary ideas far and wide led him to launch balloons containing messages and to cast bottles into the sea. This seeming eccentricity brought down upon him the most vicious attacks by the establishment of his day. This no doubt marked the beginning of the political persecution which drove him eventually into exile. His enemies' worst accusation: his behavior was puerile.

Thus I cite a greatly cherished poet, remembering how some years ago in Poland, in a meeting in solidarity with the people of Chile, I proposed (perhaps with the same puerility as Shelley) some activities which I thought might profitably replace the continual declarations which emerge from such gatherings, declarations which don't always go beyond words or beyond the people who already agree with the statements made. I suggested that instead of bemoaning Pinochet's censorship, each of us arrange to send packets of books by sea, which costs very little, to people in a position to distribute them in Chile. I know that quite a few young Chileans had a chance to read what a few of us dropped into our corner mailboxes. We're doing the same thing today, though in a different context, for the Nicaraguans.

I also suggested the possibility of perfecting short-wave broadcasts to Chile, Argentina and Uruguay. Such broadcasts would be a source of trustworthy information on all those things the governments of these countries ignore or distort. (The Malvinas war is a monumental example of how a people can be lied to even after the final disaster.) Such broadcasts might also convey the living presence of writers in exile whose voices and works would thus be able to reach thousands of listeners living under censorship of written materials, radio and television.

A More Effective Participation

IS all this childish? Or insignificant? A number of us have recorded audiocassettes, easily introduced into our countries, cassettes both literary and political in content. We have also used videocassettes to multiply a presence, or at least a nearness. A number of writers persist in writing articles which practically never make it into these countries. Why don't they break through these bars of censorship by working with video groups, now quite important in the more militant sectors of Latin America. I've just recorded a video for the fighters in El Salvador, and other *compañeros* have made videos for Guatemala, Argentina and Chile.

If the imagination is and always will be our most formidable weapon in the battle to come to power (when power is understood as a more intimate, a more effective participation in the people's struggle to discover their most authentic identity), then we *must* discover more efficient techniques than those which come out of our traditional roles as storytellers, poets, novelists and essayists, and we must do this without taking one single step backward in the work most natural to us. No matter how beautiful, how bold, how progressive our works may be in themselves, we must find new ways to introduce them into places they will never reach if we continue in our usual routines.

SLIPPING IN THE WINDOW

BY this point I trust no one will smile disdainfully if I mention possibilities such as comic strips, which might more accurately be called picture stories. Humorous drawings with satiric content—what the Anglo-Saxons call cartoons—have long since proven their political efficacy, even in countries where censorship has viciously attacked everything it considered serious, letting pass the merely comical, which can mask a seriousness people infallibly grasp.

Unfortunately, writers do not share in this art. Most of us are incapable of imagining a theme of this sort, besides which we can't draw. But the comic strip almost always supposes the collaboration of a graphic artist and a writer. This genre has magnificent practitioners in almost every country in Latin America. Yet the work of individual talents, such as Rius in Mexico, Quino in Argentina and many others you probably know, could be even more effective if writers would team up with graphic artists and expand the comic strip to dimensions which need not be inferior to those of narrative literature.

A number of years ago I stole a Mexican comic strip which included me in a most freewheeling way as one of the characters in the adventures of Fantomas, a sort of superman idolized by millions of simple readers. Friends helped me to publish a counterfeit equivalent whose true aim was to denounce the multinationals and expose the dirtiest tricks of the CIA in Latin America. The edition sold out immediately, thanks to Fantomas, who once again slipped in the window and not through the door (and with a very different goal than usual).

OTHER MEANS OF COMMUNICATION

AND what about that other plague of modernity, the photo-novel? A form with an intriguing cultural potential. If photographers were to collaborate on intelligent projects, the photo-novel could be a positive force in molding the popular imagination. But we already know the trash being printed today in magazines which stupefy millions of uneducated readers, meanwhile lining the pockets of the multinationals. And I haven't even mentioned the most fantastical, most practical weapon of all—television. Somebody will immediately point out that television, like cinema, is lock, stock and barrel owned by big business and that nobody can set foot in its sacred precincts without first undergoing a thorough brainwashing. Yet even in countries like Cuba and Nicaragua, which have channels of and for the people, it is sad to note that the programming is often conventional and facile. Why? Because all of us, writers and artists alike, have been so unadventurous that we've been incapable until now of taking by storm these strongholds out of which a true culture might emerge and start to penetrate those regions of our continent where people have nothing at all. The exceptions to this conformity may be the cinema and the theater, which in Latin America are being produced with a decidedly revolutionary accent. We need these successes badly, as we question, with some perplexity, what possible forms our own work might take.

As writers know very well, chance is our best guide through this Inferno which surrounds us. Recently, quite by accident, I happened to come across some admirable pages by Venezuelan writer Luis Britto García. Speaking at a gathering in Managua in July of last year, he addressed the problem of cultural communications in Latin America. I would like to quote this passage, which he alone could have written with such lucidity. Referring in passing to the attempt by multinationals and the mass media to crush Latin American culture by imposing their own imperialist forms, Britto García goes on to say:

> This situation creates a responsibility: the Latin American intellectual must utilize the mass media, even in countries where no immediate revolutionary perspectives are visible. Spokesmen of integrity have affirmed the right of the artist or writer to disengage his work from all militancy in favor of an aesthetic content. However, we believe that the urgency of the present moment requires of the intellectual a triple militancy: first, taking part in progressive political organizations; second, maintaining a committed stance in professional work; and third, injecting one's work into the real world of the mainstream media, thus anticipating the political revolution which will, someday, put the mass media in the hands of the people. While the political liberation may not guarantee the cultural liberation of our America, culture might lead the way to political victory.

IN ALL DIRECTIONS

WE could debate the fine points of this triple militancy. I for one don't believe that commitment should be an invariable constant in a writer's work—by no means—since pure fiction is also a leavening for revolution when it comes from an author who is recognized by his people as one of their defenders. But I do believe, with Britto García, that our job must be to open out in all possible directions, according to our talents and possibilities. To detach our work from all political activism is to turn our backs on our peoples, clinging to aesthetic decrees which are little more than dead leaves scattered into oblivion by the hurricane of our time. Yes, there are writers in Latin America who have not renounced the vanity fair of publishing houses or the adulation of privileged readers still living in ivory towers. These people have done nothing whatever (and never will) to prevent a neutron bomb from one day exploding above their heads. Perhaps they think ivory will protect them from radiation.

I'll suggest just a few more things: for example, combining popular songs with texts which might raise the music above the vulgar and sentimental conformity which remains the commercial norm. The Cuban *nueva trova* (new song) and the songs of many artists from Spain and other countries have already shown the way. Some tangos which we recorded in Paris with Argentine friends—censored, obviously, along the Rio de la Plata—are still remembered by people who heard them through clandestine channels. But I'll stop here. None of this is news to anyone, but only a way of concretizing a hope, and a desire to offer here, in the best way I know how, something more than just theories.

I'LL end with another hope, which I can't pass over. It directly concerns the vast multitude of Latin Americans exiled all over the globe. If our exile is to have any meaning, it won't come out of what has been lost, out of the pain or the nostalgia of exile. It will come instead from a total transformation of values—which can infuse exile with that strength which makes the boomerang a fearful thing: *the power of return.* Each person who has not given up that will to return can and must put his talent and imagination at the service of the people. Possibilities will open to the intellectual, not only ones such as I've sketched out here, but all the possibilities yet to be born of imagination—with its power to leap from the written page, from the novel or the poem, into reality itself, a reality more cherished and fateful than ever, the reality of Latin America, that immense book which can be written by and for all of us.

No Longer Speaking Into the Silence

HOWEVER ruthless my words may sound, I repeat: exile can be enriching to all those who remain alert and open-eyed. We will return to our lands less insular, less nationalistic, less egotistic. Yet we must start now to win that return, and the surest way is to express ourselves in work, to make contact and, indefatigably, to transmit that interior enrichment which the diaspora is giving us. This seminar of writer-friends, among whom are many exiles, has been born from the generous wish of a Spanish university to welcome me here and to reunite me with all those I love and respect.

The university will understand my gratitude when I say that my deepest hope is for this gathering to be a worthwhile moment in the task concerning us all. It's not so much this meeting which matters, but what reaches out from here to a profoundly isolated Latin America, a Latin America of millions for whom there are no gatherings, no books, no bridges.

If each of us helps to project these thoughts, using all the means at our command, we will not have come to Sitges in vain. We will not be speaking into silence.

Menéndez Pelayo International University
Sitges, Spain
September 1982

On Receiving the Rubén Darío Award

RECEIVING this award from the Sandinista people honors me
beyond expression. These words are like dark mirrors,
clouded attempts to communicate what lies far deeper and
beyond all words. This award is not just a high distinction. It
represents for me something like the end of a lengthy voyage
over the lands and seas of time, the end of a wandering life,
entering nightfall humbly, but unbroken. And as always happens in journeyings, in that eternal return where beginning
and end merge and are reconciled, I think tonight of my
childhood readings—of my awakening to poetry, both the
mediocre and the fine poetry of family and student book-
shelves. Just a few days ago in Managua I quoted a poem I
still know by heart, a poem by Gaspar Nuñez de Arce, and
tonight I see clearly that moment of my early youth when
Darío, like a bolt of lightning, forever etched his coil of fire in
my memory. Leafing through poem after poem in one of my
many books, I came across the marvel of *Colloquium of Cen-
taurs.* In a sudden illumination I discovered Rubén Darío, the
finest poetry I had ever known up to that time. Perhaps my
own fate was revealed to me then, that beautiful and harsh

sentence which condemned me to be a shepherd of words as even now I am struggling to herd that infinite flock.

I want to talk about culture, but first I had to speak of my discovery of Darío. I had to make clear what this honor means to me, this award I receive from his country at the close of my long voyage.

CULTURE in Nicaragua presents an entirely different problem from what it would in most other places. If you talk about culture as they do in Europe or in most of Latin America, you'll be wasting your breath, or at best applying formulas that might be valid elsewhere but make little sense in the reality of Nicaragua. Allow me to make a few observations of my own, without in any way claiming to exhaust a subject which by definition is inexhaustible, and difficult to define exactly. Culture is a process which brings to mind the phoenix, a dynamic both cyclical and continual, a dialectic that involves both history and reflection, a chameleon that is mental, sentimental and aesthetic, varying its colors according to the societies in which it appears. But talking about culture in the abstract doesn't get us very far. Better to approach it in the context of a specific situation. Others may discuss the history of culture, the various revolutions in culture, going back to prehistoric times, but let us speak of culture in the revolution, in this revolution, to which I am more than ever bound by love, a love for which I can never express my gratitude.

BARELY had the word *culture* arrived in Nicaragua, on July 19, 1979, than it began to be repeated, to reverberate as a constant theme, part of a highly varied plan of action. Clearly, the word *culture* here does not have the usual connotations of privilege and elitism which it has in so many circles. Nicaragua's Ministry of Culture is totally unlike its counterparts in other countries, where the idea and practice of culture has to do with hierarchy and where, at best, culture is compartmentalized, merely one among many diverse components of the social structure. You immediately sense here that the Ministry of Culture and the other agencies of government have opened up the very idea of culture. They have stripped it of that veneer of elegance which it has, say, in Western Europe. They have pushed the word *culture* into the street like an ice cream wagon or a fruit cart. With the simple, cordial gesture of someone offering a piece of fruit, they have put culture into the hands of the people. This integration of the word *culture* into the everyday vocabulary expresses what truly counts, which is not the word itself but what it contains—its explosive charge, its marvelous, delicious, actual and potential energy charge—for each inhabitant of this country. If by chance this is making any of you hungry, I'll go on to say that culture in Nicaragua is not viewed as a separate element of the social nutrition. It's not like salt or sugar, sprinkled on to add more flavor to a dish of food; it is nourishment itself.

In the final analysis, culture is manifest in every one of the initiatives, advances and achievements of the people. It is no longer the sole privilege of those who write well or sing well or paint well. That limited notion of culture has exploded. Its thousand pieces now recompose into a visible synthesis which includes innumerable wills, feelings, choices and acts.

Somebody might say this attempt at description is insufficiently precise—just the sort of criticism we'd expect from an "educated" person, somebody for whom culture is an individual acquisition, difficult to attain, hence possessed by very few, who are then set clearly apart from the masses. The *passion* for culture following the victory is a striking indication of where this revolution is heading. Justice, dignity, intellectual and artistic improvement—so much is at stake in this irreversible process of liberation. Indifferent people do not improve themselves; at best they are inculcated with the rudiments of education. But in Nicaragua you see how the masses understand the most complicated speeches and appreciate the most varied forms of art. You can see the interest people are taking in the problems of the country, in the public life. Culture is no longer an out-of-reach intellectual attainment but a state of mind, a striving by every possible means to learn and grow in the very crucible of daily life. All this is part of the cultural mobilization.

But none of this is new to any of you, though it might be to those following events here with intense interest from abroad. For you, identified with the ideas and principles of Sandino and Carlos Fonseca, the fluid border between culture and revolution, this osmosis and assimilation is simply a fact. But what is happening here is much harder to understand when the historical, intellectual and moral background is not well known. Therefore, though I'm speaking in Nicaragua to Nicaraguans, I hope my words will also reach people who have less faith in what for us is simply a given. One example: Europeans are sometimes surprised at the tremendous proliferation of poetry workshops in Nicaragua. They can hardly believe that the longing and the will to create have found so many outlets in poetry workshops all over the country. People of all ages are exercising their imaginations, enjoying that luxurious array of fruit: language itself, out of which words are picked, savored, polished and bitten into with satisfaction. This phenomenon amazes people in countries where poetry is still written in isolation, published in a handful of magazines and read by practically nobody.

It's hard for people to grasp that the writing of poetry here has absolutely nothing to do with "culture" in its usual elitist sense, but is part of a completely different culture, a culture I am doing my best to explain to the skeptical and the astonished, a culture which is revolution because this revolution is inseparable from culture.

The unconvinced may point to the traditional Nicaraguan enthusiasm for everything having to do with poetry, and I'll have to concede that it's no accident that poetry is the preferred form of cultural expression at this point in the revolution. The cultural mobilization now in full swing is rather like—if I may use an inappropriate simile—a snowball which increases in size as it rolls along. Everything I've seen so far proves I'm not mistaken. Music is one example; people attend many different concerts. And dance, with all its different styles. And the brilliant and inventive popular theater. And now plastic arts as well. The new Museum of Art of the Americas, a gift of international solidarity, should be an extraordinary stimulus to the plastic arts. Who could have dreamt of a collection of painting and sculpture such as that exhibited in the Rubén Darío Theater? Who, except those with means to travel, could ever have seen such a rich and complex parade of all the major art trends of our time? All this is culture—not a culture of isolated movements, but a culture which surges forward in one massive wave. And the irrepressible force of this wave is born of a shared thirst, that thirst for knowledge and beauty which is the same for both the people and for their leaders. Think of the publishing house Nueva Nicaragua. Barely on its feet, it has already launched a substantial and extremely fine series of books, increasingly in demand since the desire to read is now legion throughout the country— thanks to the literacy campaign.

So you see why I don't have the slightest fear that this cultural renaissance will stagnate or run out of steam. The great chameleon of art, literature, handicrafts and music will display new colors every day in the imagination of the people. But a heavy price is being paid for this cultural renewal.

I think it was a Nazi leader of the 1930s, Goering or perhaps it was Goebbels, who said: "When I hear the word 'culture' I get out my pistol." No idle threat, for when a culture is like what I see here, that culture is revolutionary, and, inevitably, the pistols will be hoisted against it. The Sandinista people are ready to face those pistols—such resolution can only emerge from plenitude, from a sense of *belonging,* of being at once an individual and part of a people—not an amorphous mass but a collectivity made up of individuals who have no desire to be isolated atoms. The creation of such atoms is the goal of many cultural programs in societies based on individualism, on the "struggle for existence," the Yankee *survival of the fittest.* This struggle is nothing other than the law of the jungle, that striving to be the richest, the most powerful or the most cultivated at the expense of any number of things, but mainly at the expense of one's fellow man.

One thing is clear: the cultural policy of Nicaragua is opening out in all conceivable directions, through every available means. I'm very moved to see that what people do here always has some moral or aesthetic incentive, is always bound up with a certain element of culture. I can see this in the speeches of the leaders, in their evident desire that everything which has to be done, however simple or repetitive, should not be just mere work, mechanical labor.

I'm especially impressed by the weekly literary supplements of the revolutionary daily papers, and with all the magazines, and radio and television programs. Each time I open one of these literary supplements I think of how, at the same moment, tucked away inside the paper, it is arriving in every corner of the country—thousands and thousands of eyes which only a short while ago did not even know the letters of the alphabet were going to read, as I would, a poem by a soldier or by a child, an article on painting or an interview with a doctor or a musician. In many families, some will never read. (Ignorance and indifference are inescapable.) But there will also be that sudden insight inspired by a story, a poem, an image—that fertile revelation which may transform a life.

Storm clouds hang over all this activity. The obstacles to disseminating culture are staggering. Time and sacrifice will be needed to overcome the miserable means of communication, the ethnic problems—everything which short-circuits the mental connections that need to be made. Taboos, prejudices, rigidified ideas must gradually be done away with. An entire negative mental apparatus (always ominous) must give way to a lucid appraisal of the revolutionary tasks at every level. Nicaragua is not Arcadia. Its highways and waterways are not like those in Switzerland. With the success of the literacy campaign, the time is now right for this cultural work to move to a deeper level in the consciousness of the masses. From one person to another, from group to group, culture is being transmitted—wherever somebody who knows something has the desire to communicate it, to make of individual attainment a shared culture. When I say shared, I don't mean a culture which is mechanically reiterated, but a seething ferment of thoughts, of feelings, and of everything this percolating mix implies in the way of discussion, polemics and failures.

Personally, I've always defended the writer's liberty to explore to the outer limits the possibilities of his work, despite the risk of being misunderstood, or of being accused of elitism, or of egotism. Nicaragua's revolutionary culture seems to me a platform for the widest possible range of ideas and sentiments. I'd be disappointed at any hint of a desire to impose a thematic or formal uniformity.

To me revolutionary culture is like a flock of birds in the open sky. The flock is always the same, but every moment its shape in the sky is changing, reassembling; its cadence shifts; the flock ascends or descends; a curve is traced in space, incessantly creating a marvelous drawing, erasing it and beginning another: and it's always the same flock and the same birds, and that, in a sense, is the culture of the birds, the exhilaration of free creation, its continual celebration.

With each new visit to Nicaragua I'm more and more convinced that the future culture of the Nicaraguan people will resemble this free form, strong in what is proper to it and at the same time open to all the winds of creation, to the liberty of planetary man.

Having attempted to cover so much ground, I hope everything which is shaky or superficial in these remarks may be overlooked. I speak of what I've seen and felt, but not in the manner of those visitors or foreign journalists who, barely in the country, feel qualified to explain and criticize anything at all, and even to make predictions concerning the future of the Sandinista revolution. I realize that all of you know this process and have lived it in far greater depth than I. Yet it may be useful for a visitor to offer his perspective, when this is done sincerely and by someone who has experienced this reality intimately and passionately before daring to speak even one word of opinion.

My sincere thanks.

Nicaragua,
February 1983

Notes

SOLENTINAME is an archipelago at the southern tip of Lake Nicaragua, near Costa Rica. There in 1966, on the island of Mancarrón, Father Ernesto Cardenal began to build a religious community among the campesinos and fisherman of the islands. Out of this community came the "primitive paintings of Solentiname," a flowering of poetry, and a large body of commentary on the Gospels. A radical interpretation of Christianity evolved into political action, as members of the community became involved in armed struggle against Somoza. A number were killed, and the community was attacked and dispersed by Somoza's National Guard in 1977. See Ernesto Cardenal *The Gospels of Solentiname*, 4 vols. (Maryknoll, N.Y.: Orbis, 1979); *The Gospel in Art by the Peasants of Solentiname*, ed. Philip and Sally Scharper (Maryknoll, N.Y.: Orbis, 1984); *Nicaraguan Peasant Poetry from Solentiname*, trans. David Gullette (Albuquerque: West End Press, 1988).

Carmen Naranjo: Born Cartago, Costa Rica, 1931. Costa Rican author of novels, short stories, poetry, plays, essays;

she is director of the publishing house, Editorial Universi-
taria Centroamericana (EDUCA).

Samuel Rovinski: Born 1936, San José, Costa Rica. Costa
Rican novelist and short story writer.

Sergio Ramírez: Born 1942, Nicaragua. Currently Vice President of Nicaragua and a member of the Sandinista National
Directorate; he became politically active against Somoza as a
university student. Leaving Nicaragua to live first in Costa
Rica, later in Germany, he devoted himself to writing fiction.
In 1975, putting writing aside, he returned from Europe to
work full time in the Sandinista struggle. Readers International has published these works in English: *To Bury Our
Fathers*, a novel (1985), and *Stories* (1986).

Ernesto Cardenal: Born 1925, Grenada, Nicaragua. From
1947 to 1949 a student at Columbia University, where he
read the poetry of U.S. moderns, especially Pound. Back in
Nicaragua he participated in a failed insurrection against the
first Somoza in 1954. Following a religious conversion, in
1957 he entered the Trappist monastery in Gethsemane, Ken-
tucky, where he and Thomas Merton talked of founding a
religious community in Nicaragua. When the rigors of the
Trappist routine rendered him seriously ill, he left the monastery without taking vows. In 1965, after study in Colombia,
Cardenal was ordained as a Catholic priest; he returned to
Nicaragua, bought a small piece of land on the island of Mancarrón, and founded the legendary community of Solentiname. After the Sandinista victory he served as Minister of
Culture. His works of poetry have been translated into many
languages.

José Coronel Urtecho: Born 1906. Leading figure in the Nicaraguan literary Vanguard movement, which took form in 1927 following his visit to the United States. This movement was based on a desire to free Nicaraguan literature from excessive dependence on European models. As translator and critic, he has been deeply involved with nineteenth- and twentieth-century modernist poetry of the United States, especially the work of Whitman, Poe, Dickinson and Marianne Moore.

Roque Dalton: Born 1933, died 1975. Salvadoran poet and revolutionary. Repeatedly imprisoned for political activities, he lived in exile in Cuba and in Czechoslovakia. In 1975 he was assassinated by a rival leftist faction. Recent translations into English: *Clandestine Poems,* ed. Barbara Paschke and Eric Weaver, trans. Jack Hirschman (San Francisco: Solidarity Press, 1984); *Poems,* trans. Richard Schaaf (Willimantic, Conn.: Curbstone Press, 1984): *Miguel Mármol,* trans. Kathleen Ross and Richard Schaaf (Willimantic, Conn.: Curbstone Press, 1987).

Carlos Martínez Rivas. Born 1924. Nicaraguan author of a single book of poems, the highly influential *La insurrección solitaria* (1953). See *Poets of Nicaragua,* comp. and trans. Steven F. White (Greensboro, N.C.: Unicorn Press, 1982).

Carlos Gardel: Famous Argentine singer of tangos.

Omar Torrijos: Died 1981. Panamanian general who came to power in a coup; he negotiated the Torrijos-Carter accord, restoring the canal to Panama. In 1981 he died in an air crash.

Tomás Borge: Born 1930, Matagalpa, Nicaragua. In 1961 one of the three original founders of the FSLN (Frente Sandinista para la Liberación Nacional); since 1979 he has been Nicaragua's minister of the interior and a member of the Sandinista National Directorate. His prison memoir of Carlos Fonseca has been translated into English by Margaret Randall: *Carlos, the Dawn Is No Longer Beyond Our Reach* (Vancouver: New Star Books, 1984). Also in English is a collection of speeches titled *Christianity and Revolution,* ed. and trans. Andrew Reding (Maryknoll, N.Y.: Orbis, 1987).

Carlos Fonseca: Born 1936, Matagalpa, Nicaragua; died 1976. One of the founders of the FSLN, he rediscovered Sandino, seeing in him a powerful unifying symbol for Nicaragua. Fonseca was the principal leader and theorist of the FSLN until his death in combat in 1976.

Miguel D'Escoto: Born 1933. A Catholic priest for over twenty-five years and a current supporter of liberation theology; he has been Nicaragua's Foreign Minister since 1979.

Claribél Alegría: Born 1924, Estelí, Nicaragua. Raised in El Salvador. An author of fiction, nonfiction, and many volumes of poetry, including *Flowers from the Volcano,* trans. Carolyn Forché (Pittsburgh: University of Pittsburgh Press, 1982), and *Woman of the River,* trans. Darwin J. Flakoll (Pittsburgh: University of Pittsburgh Press, 1989), she has also written a number of books in collaboration with her husband Darwin Flakoll, including works of political testimony.

Darwin J. Flakoll: Native of the United States; among other works in collaboration with his wife Claribél Alegría, he has edited and translated pioneering anthologies of poetry; their novel, *Ashes of Izalco,* will be published in English by Curbstone Press in 1989.

Salvador Cayetano Carpio: Respected military leader in El Salvador's guerrilla war. It was a great shock to his followers when he arranged in Managua for the assassination of a political rival. When this murder was carried out, he committed suicide.

San Francisco del Norte: Small town where a contra massacre was carried out on July 24, 1982. Fourteen campesinos were killed, four wounded, and eight kidnapped.

Daniel Ortega: Born 1945. Leader in the war against Somoza; currently President of Nicaragua and member of the Sandinista National Directorate.

Alfonso Robelo: A wealthy cotton grower and cooking oil processor in Nicaragua. He opposed Somoza and was a member of the revolutionary government, from which he resigned; he eventually became one of the three most prominent spokesmen for the contras.

Bayardo Arce: Born 1949, Managua. Actively opposed to Somoza from age sixteen, he became a leader in the guerrilla war and subsequently a member of the Sandinista National Directorate.

Archbishop of Managua: Head of the Catholic hierarchy in Nicaragua. Cardinal Miguel Obando y Bravo has long held this position, in militant opposition to the "People's Church," the Christian-based communities which support the Sandinistas. With close ties to Nicaraguan business interests, to the United States and to the C.I.A.-backed contras, Obando y Bravo has been one of the Sandinistas' most powerful opponents.

Adolfo Calero: A wealthy businessman, he was manager of Coca-Cola of Nicaragua and an active opponent of Somoza. He later became spokesman for the largest contra force, the FDN.

Augusto César Sandino. Born 1895, died 1934. Legendary Nicaraguan hero and inspiration for the Sandinista movement. Born in Niquihomo, he was raised by his mother, a poor country woman who was imprisoned for debt when Sandino was nine years old. As a young man he worked as a mechanic in Nicaragua, Honduras and Guatemala, then in the oil fields of Mexico. When the U.S. Marines invaded Nicaragua in 1926, he returned to recruit a small but heroic guerrilla army, which fought the occupation from the northern mountains of Segovia. Refusing to surrender to the marine commander, he made this declaration, which became the battle cry of the Sandinistas: "I want a free homeland or death." His impoverished army fought on for seven years until the Marines withdrew in 1933, having set up the National Guard under the first Somoza. In Managua to negotiate a peace agreement with Nicaraguan President Sacasa, Sandino was captured by the National Guard on the steps of the Presidential Palace following this meeting. Taken to the edge of town he was brutally shot, with two of his generals, Francisco Estrada and Juan Pablo Umanzor.

Pulgarcito is the Spanish equivalent of Tom Thumb.